BEYOND BLOOD

BEYOND BLOOD

REGINALD A. SMITH

Beyond Blood by Reginald Smith © 2024

All rights reserved. No part of this book may be reproduced, stored in a retrieval system, or transmitted by any means, electronic, mechanical, photocopying, recording, or otherwise, without written permission from the publisher or author, except as permitted by U.S. copyright law. No patent liability is assumed with respect to the use of the information contained herein. Although every precaution has been taken in the preparation of this book, the publisher and author assume no responsibility for errors or omissions. Neither is any liability assumed for damage resulting from the use of information contained herein.

Unless otherwise indicated, all Scripture quotations are taken from the Holy Bible, New Living Translation, copyright 1996, 2004. Used by permission of Tyndale House Publishers, Inc., Wheaton, Illinois 60189.

Scriptures marked KJV are taken from the KING JAMES VERSION (KJV): KING JAMES VERSION, public domain.

Scripture taken from the New King James Version®. Copyright © 1982 by Thomas Nelson. Used by permission. All rights reserved

Scriptures marked NIV are taken from the NEW INTERNATIONAL VERSION (NIV): Scripture taken from THE HOLY BIBLE, NEW INTERNATIONAL VERSION ®. Copyright© 1973, 1978, 1984, 2011 by Biblica, Inc.™. Used by permission of Zonderva.

ISBN:979-8-218-40193-1

Editor: Daphney M. Chaney [Emerge Editing & Writing]
Interior Design: Marvin D. Cloud

Printed in the United States of America

For ordering information: Contact Reginald Smith at www.esyntrek1.com

Dedication

To my mother, my first love Norma J. Smith and daddy Richard A. Smith (Deceased) Words cannot express how grateful I am for you allowing me to be apart of your family. You may have had other options, but you chose me. You loved me like I was born from you and never showed any partiality. You afforded me opportunities that many did not have. I am the man I am because of you.
I am eternally grateful.
– Love Reggie

To Richard and Norma Smith

In the depths of my heart, a love so pure,
For my mother and father, forever endure.

Their guiding hands and unwavering care,
A bond so strong, beyond compare.

Like a gentle breeze, my mother's embrace,
Comfort and warmth, in every trace.

Her love, like a beacon, lighting my way,
Through every storm, come what may.

And my father, a pillar of strength and might,
His wisdom and guidance, a guiding light.

With every step, he's there by my side,
Teaching me courage, filling me with pride.

Together they've shaped me, nurtured my soul,
With love and devotion, they've made me whole.

Their sacrifices, countless and true,
A testament to the love they imbue.

So, here's to my mother, and my father so dear,
In this heartfelt poem, my love is clear.

Forever grateful, forever I'll be,
For the love of my parents, eternally. *Forever your son.*

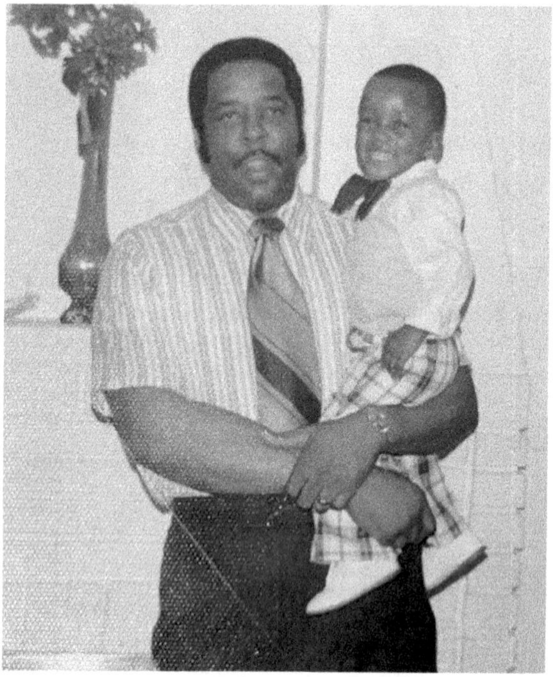

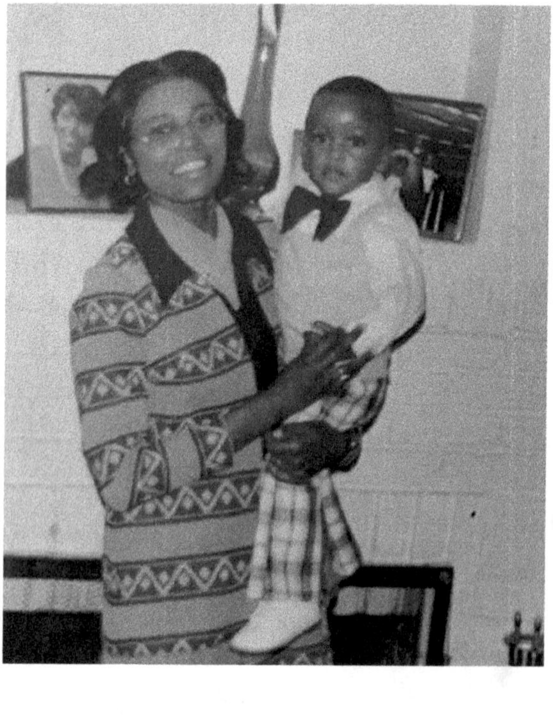

Dedications Continued.....

To my wife Diana L Smith, there are not many women like you on this planet. You are loving, giving, tenacious and smart in every thing that you do. Everything and everyone you encounter are better because of it. You are and continue to be a blessing. You are the glue and the bond that keeps the family intact. You love me unconditionally. You are my ride or die; my Wonder Woman and my Showtime. Thank you for your support, and realness. Thank you for rocking with me. - *Love,* **HBO**

To Jaye K. Reynolds (Mom) and **Homer** (Champ) **Thornton** (Father, deceased) I want you to know that although giving me up may have been hard and unconventional, it was the best decision that you could have made. It didn't mean you didn't love me, but you loved me enough to give me a better life. One that was and is filled with endless opportunities. I am so grateful mom, that we had the opportunity to reconnect. You are a breath of fresh air on the cloudiest of days. Champ sorry that we missed one another. But there is a reason and season for everything and hopefully we will see each other in eternity.

Acknowledgments

Renarde Smith (Brother #1-My day 1) Todd White (Brother #2) Donniel Cundiff (Brother #3) Jonathan Cundiff (Brother #4). I've always wanted siblings and a band of brothers. You guys don't even understand how it made my heart glad to see you all together in Vegas for the first time as if you had been together forever. That was a feeling even to this day that I can't explain. I love you guys and can't wait until our guys' trip.

To Veronica (Sis) I never got the chance to meet you, but the fact that you were looking for me makes me smile. It's bittersweet. The fact that I never had the chance to call you sis or to hear your voice hurts but there is a reason for everything, right? You would have loved me, and I no doubt would have loved you. I pray to meet you on the other side.

To my kids, you guys have loved and accepted me from the very beginning, and I am so grateful for your love and support.

Reggie Smith Jr. (you will always be the better half of me, I got you to the end, I promise).

Taleah Redd, thanks for always laughing at my jokes. I love you. Tiyona Wright, I can't wait until we finally work out! I love you. Derrick Redd (and the beat downs in madden keep coming. I love you.

Akeem Wright (You gone learn today).

Ma Thelma Bonner, the best mother-in-law on the planet, I love you and yes, I know I can't give her back!

Sherrie (Sis) Love you big sis, except when we play spades.

Troy B, Iron sharpens Iron.

Mike Hill (Brother RIP) I miss you so much man.

Kenneth Bonner (Thanks bro for your love and support. You are a true man after God's own heart.

Pastor Ji Nelson (Thanks for always keeping it real and just listening when I needed it the most).

Pastor Larry Shelby (My constant rock. We talk about those things that many don't dare to speak about. I love you dad).

Curtis Webster (40 years of friendship).

Anthony Rodriguez (Brother from another mother).

Brian Simpson (My day 1, Bone Brother B).

Indesha Redd (One who inspires) we talked about this years ago that eventually my work would be on display. Well this is the beginning of more to come.

Javanyce Harris (Always my daughter, no matter what. Love you).

Mother Frank (I love you more than words can say, one of my biggest supporters since I can remember, all my love to you).

Gran Gran-Hey Bay Bay, I miss you so much. You would be proud of me. I'm still trying to be the best I can be. (RIP)

Aunt Mille, Uncle Chuck, and Uncle Chubby, thank you for accepting me, you really don't know how much of an impact that has had on me. I love you more than you know.

To Mr. and Mrs. Rodriguez and Mr. and Mrs. Alvarado. You were my home away from home. You guys do not know how much it felt to be accepted into your home when my father died. I was secretly struggling, but you all helped me in ways I could never repay you.

Chucky and Diana Alvarado. I love you guys, my brother and sister, always.

To Daphney Chaney. Thank you so much for helping this vision come to fruition. I had sight, but you definitely had the vision. When I grow up I want to be just like you.

Contents

Introduction	*1*
Chapter One	
Humble Beginnings	5
Chapter Two	
Confronting The Child Within	17
Chapter Three	
Adopted	27
Chapter Four	
Parental Responsibility	41
Chapter Five	
Six Degrees Of Separation	49
Chapter Six	
My Brother's Keeper	61
Chapter Seven	
Faulty Construction	71
Chapter Eight	
Unprocessed Pain	85
Conclusion	*95*

Appendices:		*101*
	Family Secrets	*103*
	Adoption	*107*
Notes		*113*
Biography		*115*

Introduction

I've been gifted in articulating words in such a fashion that poetry flows from my very essence. It is a way of communication that comes as an easier way to express my innermost thoughts. Therefore, you will see poetry peppered throughout this book. The idea for this book first came to me and I started writing as memories surfaced. Eventually, life with its busyness happened and I put it on the shelf for a while.

When I met my biological mother, she gave me some details about my biological father. I shared several things that I learned about him through my research and from others. I also shared what I'd learned about several of my other biological relatives with her and how we seemed to live a six degree of separation type of life. Afterward, she also mentioned that I should write a book. That served as more confirmation for me as I had already begun journaling my adoption story.

I was speaking to a friend who mentioned his adoption, he wanted some insight from me, because he knew that I had already begun the search for my biological parents. His story was so touching that I told him it sounded like a book. In one of our other conversations, I mentioned that we should try to collaborate and do a compilation project.

He wanted to invite two more friends who were also coming to grips with the truth of being adopted. Although parallel, our stories were still different. Therefore, I agreed to the collaborative book writing project. He and I began sharing our stories with our ghostwriter/editor. As more time passed, two of the four aspiring authors were not as ready to engage in writing the book as we were. That left us with two. Life kept taking us in different directions, but I was ready to push forward with telling my story and adding this informative memoir to my list of accomplishments. Writing and reading these pages added to my self-reflection and inner healing. Therefore, this solo project was born.

Watching the movie Antoine Fisher and becoming absorbed in his adoption story pierced my heart in such a way that I longed to trace my roots. It was the fire that ignited the words that you will read over the following pages. Throughout this book, I will use the terms "adoptive parents" and "biological parents" to differentiate for the sake of the reader. My use of these terms in no way diminishes the role or importance of my "adoptive parents." They did more than just raise me; they loved me as their very own. Because in their hearts, that is exactly who I am (their very own). They are my parents, and I will forever love and acknowledge them as that.

The framework of family is as complex as it is beautiful. Adoption helps people to see beyond blood. The scope of the family must take on a broader sense, in that family is a cohesive bond through relationships intertwined with acceptance and responsibility.

Whether a child is raised in a loving family or a toxic one, the news of adoption is never easy. One is often left with many unanswered questions. I know what it means to try to cultivate a healthy family on the heels of unhealthy emotions. Furthermore, most adoptive parents struggle with how the adopted child will view them in lieu of finding their biological parents. Unfortunately, I am also acquainted with being in the middle of trying to please everyone. However, I'm sure, parents don't think about the child in the process, instead it turns into a self-protection or defense type of mechanism. Understanding both the biological parents and the adoptive parent's proclivities towards possessiveness, aids in keeping balance and boundaries. This is important so that all parties realize it is the child who has dealt with the most emotional aspect of the process.

Although my adoption story is unique, it did not lessen the effects of rejection, abandonment, or the feelings of being orphaned. I grew up in a loving environment, and still, deep inside, my soul was fragmented. I didn't even notice until my teen years when my "adoptive" father passed away. Grief hit me like a ton of bricks, and what was once dormant, emerged like a tsunami. That loss was the catalyst that caused me to spiral downward. I'd always known that I was adopted, but the reality finally set it and I struggled with knowing my identity. I learned about my adoption by accident at the age of seven. I didn't comprehend the full extent of it, and no one in my family ever made me feel less than a blood-born "Smith."

I was afraid of meeting my biological parents and feared facing additional rejection. I was also concerned with what the family would think of me telling my story, but the response has been met with great support. My adoptive mom never objected to me wanting to find my biological family, and for that I am grateful. I don't want to give too much away in this introduction, but you will feel my heart on every page.

I pray the pages of *Beyond Blood* will speak to the child still living inside the adult and become the impelling force towards healing. It is my hope that it will also become a call to action for families to move beyond the past and courageously build toward a brighter future. Remember, it doesn't matter where we start, it is how we reposition ourselves to finish. We reproduce after our own kind, our children will ultimately become what we model before them. Lastly, I pray this book challenges the way you think regarding family, and the lessons contained herein will pass from generation to generation.

Chapter One
Humble Beginnings

Antwone Fisher is the touching story about a young sailor who never dealt with the roots of his volatile behavior. As I watched this movie, it touched me in ways that I could have never fathomed. Each scene reverberated in my soul. I was moved immensely by this film. As the film progressed, Antwone was forced to confront his painful past and dig deep into his horrific childhood. My own pain came to the surface, and tears streamed down my face. Although I could not relate to the abuse he suffered at the hands of his foster parents, his violent behavior struck a chord. Growing up, I had no idea that unprocessed pain was the core of my violent outburst.

When my adoptive father (the only father I'd known passed away), I wasn't emotionally fortified to deal with the level of grief that I felt. Not only did it leave me feeling empty, but the news of my adoption also came rushing back to my mind. I'd known about the adoption since I was about seven years old. But at that age, it didn't register. I couldn't fully process it, especially since my childhood was filled with everything any kid could want and desire.

It was like yesterday that my father sent me into the bedroom to get some paperwork out of the safe. My dad was a numbers guy. He loved teaching me about numbers, counting, math, etc. He taught me to open the safe in our home in case of emergencies. I was in the third grade and was so happy that my dad wanted to give me the responsibility of opening the safe. It made me feel like a big boy. I felt like no other third grader on the planet had that responsibility. When he told me to get something for him, I immediately got up from playing with my Tonka trucks, ran into the room and got into the prone position. With one hand on my cheek, I tried to remember the numbers. Remembering them would prove to him that I was really taking this responsibility seriously. I said them out loud as I listened to the click of the dial. Thirty-two to the right, sixteen to the left, and four to the right. A smile came over my face, as I thought, "Mission accomplished."

I began looking for the pieces of paper my father sent me to retrieve. As I was moving paper around in the safe, I stumbled across what I would eventually come to know as carbon paper. I'd never seen paper like that before; it was thin and very fragile; therefore, if you moved it around too much, it would tear easily. I saw a bunch of writing in black ink, but a name stood out that caught my attention. I began to sound out the words just as we were taught in Ms. Sullivan's class.

She would have been very proud of me. I sat up in Indian style and started to pronounce each letter. La-wre-nce, La-wre-wre-nce Thor-ton. After forty or so seconds of sounding out each letter, I was ready to put it together. "Lawrence Thornton, hmmmmm, Lawrence Thornton." I closed the safe, forgetting what my father sent me to get and trotted into the kitchen still holding the paper I found. My dad was smoking his Tareyton cigarettes while my mother was washing dishes and preparing dinner.

I walked into the kitchen and asked, "Who is Lawrence Thornton?" I remember seeing my mother turn off the water faucet, and my father took a puff of his cigarette, he blew smoke out the side of his mouth, and grabbed the ashtray and put it out.

He said, "I think it's time."

I can't recall the entire conversation, but I remember hearing, "Reggie, you were adopted."

I asked, "Do I have any brothers and sisters?"

My mother replied, "Yes, but we do not know where or who they are. We adopted you because we love you and want you always to know that." My mother reinforced her statement, "you are loved, and we love you, Reggie."

As I picked up the thin piece of paper, I asked, "Is this my name?"

"That was your name," replied my mother, "but we changed it so that you would have your father's last name and be a part of our family."

After the conversation with my parents, it was hard to reconcile "adoption" in my mind. Still going over it in my head, I remember, saying my prayers before bed and asking God not to take my real parents from this earth until I had a chance to see them. I stayed on my knees for a couple of seconds, and like most kids, I just laid in the bed, made some shadow figures with my hands, put the covers over my head, and went to sleep.

The following day, I got dressed for school, and decided to tell my friends that I was adopted. I've always been a person to do things just to spark reactions from people. I wanted to see their reactions and hear what they'd have to say. At some point in class, I wrote a letter in crayon to my friend Carnell, I saw his eyes open wide, and he passed the note to a couple more people, and within minutes half of the room knew the biggest hit of the 80s.

All they could say was, "Wow," as if they really understood what it meant, and after a few minutes and questions from my peers, it was back to work. No one ever brought it up again, and neither did I. But for years I constantly looked for anyone that resembled me. Whenever I met a new friend or a girl I liked, I'd ask the question in my head, "Is this my cousin, my brother, or my sister?" While playing sports, I wondered if my competitors and I were related. Although the pain was inaudible to the ears of those around me, the barrage of voices and questions in my head rang aloud. In fact, I couldn't identify it as pain. All I knew was that covered under the beautiful life I had, a part of me felt broken.

My parents didn't offer any additional information. And the reason I didn't bother asking any more questions was because my parents made sure that my brother and I had the best life possible. We were raised in a middle-class neighborhood and attended private school. Our parents were educated and hard working. They set great examples for us, were very involved in our lives, and kept us active in sports. We even enjoyed lots of family time and plenty of family vacations. My childhood was good, and I most certainly felt loved. I have very fond memories of my brother and I playing for hours with GI Joes, Transformers, and Tonka Trucks.

I never knew the voids from those unanswered questions at age seven would resurface and greatly impact my life, until my dad (adoptive) passed away. His death left me without a father. I looked into the mirror one day and realized I didn't know my real identity. It is uncanny how one moment of pain can trigger a lifetime of suppressed emotions. Losing my dad caused me to become angry, mad, and hurt. Growing into young adulthood, I'd sabotage relationships to avoid the pain of someone else leaving me.

While growing up, I didn't mention my adoption to my cousins or other relatives because I was afraid of hearing things like, "That is why you are adopted!" or "You are not really one of us." What appears as harmless jesting, joking, or even the results of retaliation and revenge through verbal onslaughts is the cause of millions of suicides and depression among children and teens.

Regardless of how much you attempt to teach children that bullying and teasing often stem from within the walls of an insecure frame; the receivers' wounds typically go deeper than the sender's scars. This malicious abuse often masks pain, by revealing another's. One of my older cousins knew that I was adopted, however, he kept it a secret. I don't know why, but I applaud him for it. I was adopted at nine months old; therefore, the cousins my age and younger had no idea.

As an adult, I have had to work through much of the manifestations of rejection and abandonment. But not before walking head-on into a destructive path of failed relationships, distrust, promiscuity, and avoidance. The feelings of low self-worth were masqueraded in arrogance and pride. I remember once, being vulnerable enough to share my adoption with a woman I was dating.

Unfortunately, she wasn't mature enough to handle the weight of that information. Inherently, some of the things that bind us to another person are the very things we strive to separate from. Brokenness often latches on to brokenness. Therefore, instead of recognizing her inability to help me through my pain, I poured my heart into a soul that was already bleeding. After an argument one day she shouted, "That's why you are adopted and no one wanted you!"

The pain of her words seemed unbearable. They haunted me for years. I realized, not only was I grieving my father (adoptive), but I was also grieving the thoughts of who I was supposed to be. Unfortunately, I didn't know who that was. At that point, I realized that two dads were missing. My adoptive father who passed away and my biological father who I considered a loss, because he was absent from my life. Tears filled my pillow at night as tormenting questions about my biological father plagued my mind. Why? Where are you? Why didn't you want me? What kind of work do you do? What should I do with my own life? Are you somewhere out there searching for me, or am I a faded memory? I had so many questions that this poem poured from my soul:

Dear Dad,

I would like to know
whose decision it was
to put me up for adoption
Before the decision was made,
were there any other options?

Don't get me wrong,
I am not complaining,
because my transition was smooth,
and I found myself placed
with a family
that took me in as their own
and I became one of them.

They made a vow
to treat me the same,
while giving me their last name.
My question is,
was this a joint effort,
who had the final say so?

It took me several years
to locate my biologicals, only to find out
that I missed you by several months.

That's sad because I had questions,
a lot of questions that needed answered,
And like cancer
it was eating me up from within.

The only thing I had of you
was an obituary.
And to be honest
it was downright scary,
how we favored,

The stance, the pose,
the flare in the nose,
all those little things
that identified you,
were like me looking
in the mirror seeing my twin.

Not only did I favor you,
but it was also like you
created me with no help at all.
It got worse, I found out that
we shared the same passions,
coupled by our taste in fashion.

That left me in shock and dismay,
there was no possible way
that your traits both good and bad,
would turn out to be my blessings
and a curse.

We wore the same rings
on the same hand,
and chains on the wrist,
If you were still here,

there could be no way
that anyone could dismiss
that I was your son.

For years, I would unknowingly
stop by the same places
that you would visit,
and on numerous occasions
I heard,
"You look like, or you remind me of…
or hey, is your father named Champ?"

My response would always be
No, because I truly did not know.
I never knew what to really say,
and things really set me back
to find out that we lived in the
same little city, just blocks away.

Your friends of my close friends
were also my friends
and no one ever put two and two together,
so, I guess 2+2 doesn't equal 4.

How could they see you
and see me and not connect we?
Let me share this with you,
when I found out that I was adopted,
deep on the inside, I struggled with who I was.
Asking the age-old rhetorical question, why?

And as I got older I dealt with the rejection.
Every time I looked in the mirror
I struggled with my reflection,

because I could not identify
it with anyone.

The rejection became an infection
and at times I lost my direction,
afraid of what I would become
or if I would end up alone with no connection
to my bloodline.

So, with all of my accomplishments
and achievements,
I had a void lying deep inside of me
coupled with the fears
followed by long nights of pillows
drenched in tears.
Why?
Because I felt that you didn't want me.
Well, did you?
Would I have been too much?
Was I too much for you to handle?
Where was your voice?
Did you ever stop to see the vision?

Was I ever in your future?
I would have loved to be the fly on the wall
to see how you handled the decision.
Did you ever wonder about the possibility
of what could have been?

In the words of Brian McKnight,
"Did I ever cross your mind?"
As you took your last breath,
was I in your thoughts?

I was told that you looked for me,
but my name had changed,
on paper I was not linked to you,
But our DNA would have painted
a different view.

I guess I'll never know your thoughts,
What was on your mind and heart?
Could you have honestly said
you did your part?

I'm not angry, confused,
or disappointed in the decision,
because in hindsight,
it was the best decision
that was ever made.

I am the person I am today
because of that decision,
and I don't fault you at all.

Your Son, RS—

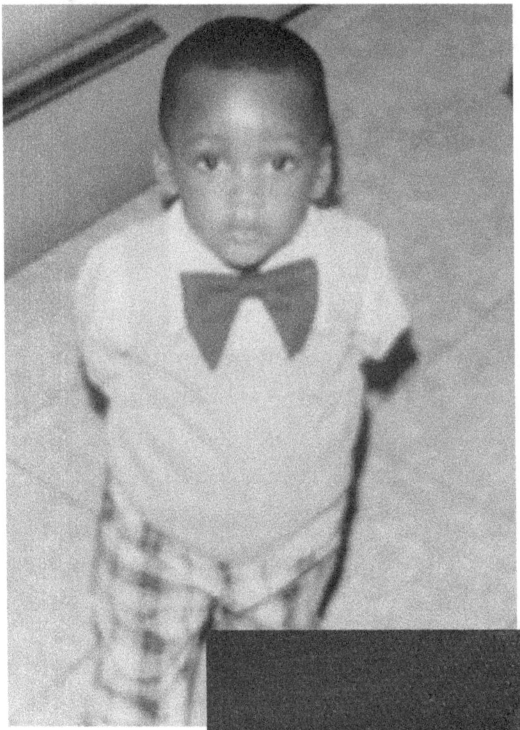

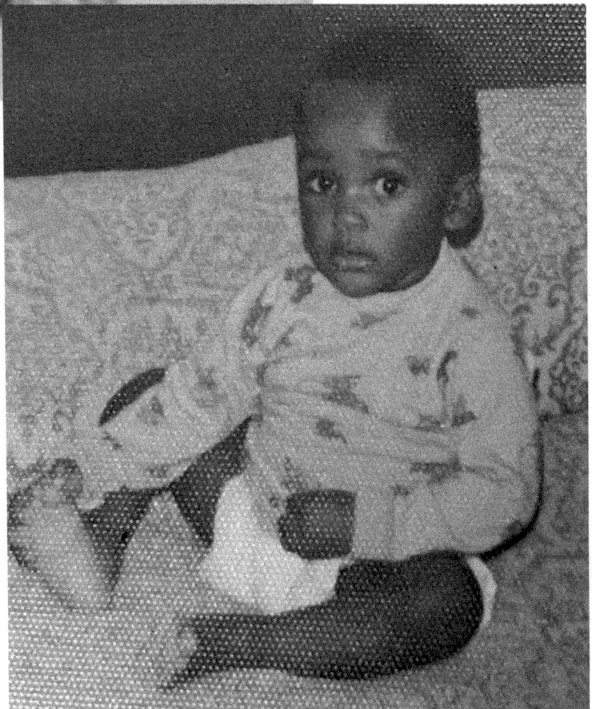

In penning this memoir, revisiting these moments has brought up the painful part of this process, yet I know this story is greater than nostalgia. As I grew, I kept waiting for time to ease the pain. I was told being in God would help, and I'd find my identity in Christ. It is true that Christ gives us a new identity. However, I couldn't perceive anything new while I was still living under the old, fragmented version of me. A man's relationship with his father is the cornerstone of his relationship with himself. Every other relationship is a byproduct of those. Psychologists agree that a father's significance in child rearing, especially in boys, is vastly unique from that of a mother.

Although my dad (adoptive) gave me a good life, there were things about myself I still needed to discover. There are things I wished he'd been able to reveal to me. Losing him robbed me of that opportunity, or so I thought, until I came of age and took charge of my own emotional well-being. But it was years before that manifested. Still, during the most formable years of adolescence, I struggled with self-defeating thoughts. What if I found my biological dad, and he'd choose not to accept me? I'd needed to run back to the only arms to hold me and reassure me that I was and am still good (my adoptive father). If that happened, I'd need him to tell me that I wasn't just something to discard. I can picture him wiping my tears as his embrace would reaffirm my identity and purpose. Instead, I had to deal with the two losses that fractured my self-image.

Chapter Two
Confronting The Child Within

My being adopted seemed to be hushed around the house. But for me, the sound forever echoed in my soul. I couldn't help but wonder if I resembled my biological mom or dad. I was curious about my cousins and other relatives. I wanted to know if I came from a big family. I wondered if I'd find dating difficult. What if I dated a relative, how would we know. I noticed the gap between my teeth, and every time I saw someone with a gap between their teeth, I wondered if we were related. Funny, but I even wondered if actor Eddie Murphy and I were kin. As a child, the thought of being related to him was thrilling! He was funny, famous, and rich. In my child-like mind, that would have been pretty cool!

I'm the kind of person who must know the genesis of everything. I was highly bothered that I could not trace my lineage in my head. By the time I was adopted, my parents weren't sure if they could have kids, but three years later my baby brother was born. I knew he would have no issues identifying himself as theirs. He could easily see a resemblance. The funny thing is, if I hadn't known that I was adopted, I'd fit right in as well.

Despite the barrage of questions, I've never questioned my parents' love for me. I'm grateful to have been reared in such a loving family. They've never made any difference between my brother and me. Unfortunately, there are children who face unfair and partial treatment because they are not biologically blood-related. Whether they are adopted or stepchildren, many face rejection, abandonment, and abuse. In lieu of my situation, I would be remiss if I failed to offer the advice of not adopting, fostering, or signing up to raise children, if your heart isn't open enough to feel beyond "blood." Do not take on the privilege of rearing children. I used the word privilege rather than challenge because it is an honor. The Bible says that children are a blessing. When a person takes on the role of a parent, and is not emotionally well, it can place an unfair burden upon a child. The damage can seem irreparable to an innocent heart who just wants a place to belong. I included an appendix on adoption at the end of this book to provide more information.

"This is my beloved Son in whom I'm well pleased."
(Matthew 3:17 KJV)

There is nothing like the approval of a father. I expended what seemed like an eternity attempting to find approval in anyone who would give it to me. When my son was born, I wanted to be sure that he'd never feel any of the voids that I felt. I developed a strong sense of protection for him. At the time of his birth, in my mind, I understood that he and I were all we had. So, if something happened to him, I didn't have anyone to carry on my legacy. Therefore, I made it a point to protect him in every way possible. He could at least carry on the family name. As I pondered these thoughts, it was overwhelming, especially because I was left feeling as if I'd been robbed of carrying on my lineage.

In addition, I've always felt like I had to prove myself to everyone that I encountered. I feared rejection so strongly that I went out of my way for others to see the value that I failed to see within myself. I tried to do it without revealing my deep insecurities. The wounds were so obscure that even I didn't recognize them easily. I couldn't identify the aching to be loved in my soul because my parents and my brother loved me dearly. Therefore, the void within me didn't appear to make sense. I didn't know at the time that pain from the womb establishes a set pattern of behavior. When a baby is born, the baby is instantly placed on the mother's chest to develop bonding. It's called skin-to-skin contact.

My therapist helped me to realize missing that moment of being welcomed in my mother's arms and nestled under the warmth of her breast created a void within me. I was robbed of receiving the stability that is shown to calm and relax a baby. It is also shown to regulate the baby's heart rate and breathing, and helps them better adapt to life outside of the womb. There is a connection between mother and baby that gives the foundation for all other connections made in life. But well before my actual entrance into the world, the first bonding occurred. For forty weeks, my tiny fetus grew in my biological mother's uterus. The bonding at birth was supposed to be a continuum of a spiritual, physical, and psychological miracle. For forty weeks, I'd already adapted to her sound, smell, and emotions. Therefore, long before putting me up for adoption, I may have been rejected in the womb.

I never asked my biological mom how being pregnant affected her, or if she wanted a baby? When you read about our meeting and connection, you will get the full picture of why she chose adoption. However, I was taught on a spiritual level, that babies can feel rejection in the womb. Consequently, my issues started well before I took my first breath outside of the womb. Studies show that women are often told how to care for their bodies with proper nutrition and rest, but until recently has mental health come into the picture. An unwanted pregnancy can create feelings of insecurity and rejection in the fetus. The range of emotions that a baby can pick up on is extremely vast. I was adopted at nine months and my parents thought they'd adopted me early enough to avoid those negative feelings being formed, but the void was already there. My adoptive mom told me that I cried in her arms when she first received me for a week straight after the adoption. She could sense that I missed the arms and faces of those at the adoption center. Again, going from void to void even as a baby, created a cycle of wanting to belong before I could even form words or take my first step.

I do not want to place the entire blame of my insecurities on the adoption, but I strongly believe it largely contributed to it. There is a spiritual aspect to everything that we face in life. Long before therapy, the effects of non-bonding with my maternal mother had effects that I couldn't reconcile in my mind. There is always a root to our behavior. We are a much wiser generation, and I am happy to see so many taking charge of their mental health. Yet still a vast majority negate how beneficial therapy is to emotional well-being. It is helping me realize that a lot of my personal and marital issues stemmed from my childhood adoption. Also, I've been able to uncover roots that I wasn't aware existed.

Going back to my infancy, my biological mother never held me. She didn't get to see me before I was taken away, and didn't know how crucial those first moments were to my development. According to the full report my adoptive mother was given, I cried for several weeks when I was first placed in foster care. Then, by the time I had gotten used to the scent and comfort of my foster mother, I was disconnected from her through adoption. As a baby, I had no idea, but my soul and spirit knew that the arms that held me were no more. My spirit was going through all kinds of different transitions. Look at the pattern: First, I was disconnected in the womb through an unwanted pregnancy. Second, I was disconnected from my mom by the absence of a skin-to-skin connection. Third, I was disconnected from the foster home, and finally growing into adulthood, it led to me disconnecting from everything in life. My disconnection was different. It wasn't that I was withdrawn and didn't enjoy relationships because I did. It was my actions in those relationships that revealed the voids and insecurities in my life. Although I cherished relationships, I often built walls. I was afraid of rejection and projected that onto my intimate partners. Lacking true connecting skills, my relationships served more as validation of who I was as a man. My extreme guards were my method of self-preservation. I wanted to avoid rejection at all costs.

It all makes perfect sense when I look back over my life. I had every reason as a kid to be happy. I had loving parents who treated my brother and me like kings. We were given opportunities for success, enjoyed family bonding, and had a very close-knit family. I remember my dad saying that he didn't want us to have children all over the place, but if we did, we were to behave responsibly and be sure they were taken care of. He consistently reiterated the need for "Smith" men to be responsible. He said things like, "That's what Smith men do!" He was a no-nonsense kind of man. He said what he meant and meant what he said. He valued friendships, family, and hard work.

He prided himself on making sure that we were prepared for everything in life, including his departure if God were to call him home. He instilled strength and accountability in us. He also mentioned his priority was to be sure my mother was well provided for. In fact, my mother told me when they were in the process of adopting, as they glanced over the children, he looked at me and said, "he is the one I want." It's like he had some kind of insight and foresight to know to choose me. Somehow, he just knew. He looked into my mother's eyes and told her that I would take care of her if something ever happened to him.

My adoptive dad taught me everything that I know. He was a manly man in every sense of the word. But even in his masculinity, he was vulnerable enough to embrace us with hugs and to verbally convey his love for us, therefore, for me to emerge as a fragile, insecure young man, had nothing to do with my upbringing, but everything to do with what had already taken place in the spirit and in my soul.

I hid behind those insecurities and created an alter ego that I could relate to and identify. I became the tough guy. I didn't share or express too many emotions. And I'd sabotage relationships to avoid the sting of rejection. I'd go out of my way to hear compliments because they served as words of affirmation for me. I didn't know my own worth, so I made people overcompensate in relationships to prove their affection for me. When men do this, it causes women to compromise their values. At the expense of their self-worth, they lose themselves just to be with a man who is unable to give them the love that they truly deserve.

Rejection manifests itself in many ways. At times it is unique to the individual and the individual circumstance. In my life, rebellion to authority wasn't my issue. However, on an inner level my self-esteem, confidence, and identity suffered. Once again, I kept hearing that I should know my identity in Christ. I earnestly tried, but for me attempting to find my physical identity in an unseen spiritual entity didn't work. I just didn't understand that math. Reading the Bible and attending church helped in other ways but, not in the form of identifying who I was.

I did well in school and progressed in life. However, my relationships continued to suffer from my loss of identity. I couldn't shut down the nagging thoughts and questions. Over and over in my head, I asked, *Why didn't they keep me? Why me? Why, why, why?*

Furthermore, I wanted to know if I had any siblings, if so, were they kept or also put up for adoption? I questioned if they were close to one another, if they knew about me, and if they ever tried to find me? Because of my need to be accepted and feel a part of something, these questions heightened my fear of rejection and anxiety. In my warped way of thinking, I've always wanted to be selected, not rejected. So, I did whatever I could to ensure it was a reality. I went the extra mile in sports and was very competitive. I overachieved and at times underachieved.

Rejection doesn't leave us with a balance, instead it tips from one end of the scale to the other. It can swing from the insecurity of being rejected to the fear of being rejected. There is no middle ground. Both extremes manifest in behavior patterns that can be toxic. It leads to promiscuity, self-sabotage, extreme self-criticism, feelings of low worth, and anything to prove your worth.

The truth is I just wanted to belong. And again, my family was very loving. I have older cousins and at no time did any of them make me feel like I wasn't a "Smith" through blood relation. We'd emerge from disagreements and periods of not speaking like most families do, but without the damaging words and gossip that often destroy relationships. I can't think of a time that I ever heard, "that's why you aren't one of us" or "You are adopted!" That speaks volumes as to the strong family values and ties that were instilled within the bloodline of the "Smiths."

The turmoil I found myself in again, was all inner conflict. I mentioned that my adoptive dad passed away when I was 15. And as I grew into adulthood, the inner battles surfaced and resurfaced again and again. At age 50, I'm just now learning to fight rejection and abandonment through counsel and therapy. I've learned in order to be victorious against this, that I must reject and cancel the lies I've believed. We all know that perception can become reality. Therefore, I somehow believed that I was unworthy of love, although I longed deeply for that attachment. The little boy inside of me is finally being released from the bondage of emotions that I experienced in the womb.

Another part of healing from abandonment, rejection, and the spirit of the orphan is forgiveness. I had to forgive my biological parents for releasing me from their care. I used the word "release" instead of giving up because giving up would indicate that they gave up on me, on the other hand, to release me, means that they gave me another chance at life. I had to realize that they released me from their responsibility. Instead of rejecting me, they rejected their parental rights. The lies we believe can form impenetrable barriers if we allow them to. Thankfully, God has already made provision for healing for each of us. It takes courage to confront deeply rooted feelings and emotions; therefore, forgiveness was also extended to myself. I forgave "me" for what I believed and allowed to fester in my soul. Forgiving little offenses may come easy, but depending upon the severity of the pain, forgiveness may take a repeated effort. Pray and seek the help of a professional if necessary.

I wasn't an orphan in the sense of being without parents, yet the spirit somehow found a place in my soul. I'm no authority on the subject, therefore; this topic is based on my personal journey. In the spiritual aspect, the soul of an orphan is always seeking approval, purpose, and satisfaction in life. That fulfillment is sought in relationships with people, rather than a deep personal relationship with Christ. I mentioned in the first chapter how losing my adoptive father caused negative emotions to surface. Feelings of fatherlessness are almost identical to those listed above for rejection. Statistics prove that young men without fathers are more than likely to engage in criminal activity, be incarcerated, abuse alcohol and other substances, drop out of school, and or abandon their own children.

I'm grateful that none of those statistics proved to be my truth. Unfortunately, my soul remained orphaned as my mind consistently struggled with a fractured identity. Feeling orphaned impacts our self-perception. It can cause us to feel rejected by people who are not really rejecting us. It also conceals manhood and womanhood under childish behaviors. I watched my self-worth crumble beneath my good looks, charm, wit, and perfectionism. Insecurity caused me to try to earn love, instead of authentically receiving it.

There are no quick fixes for emotional wounds; healing takes time. Use your time wisely and avoid dragging others into your pain in the process. This is easier said than done, as we all have the desire to love and be loved. Therefore, extend grace to those who may be used to plant seeds of faith, pluck up roots of decay, and bear the burden of your journey. Heal on purpose so that your children and their children aren't affected by generational curses.

Chapter Three
Adopted

While my parents did not shield me from the fact that I was adopted, they did not offer too much information concerning my biological parents at the time. They did the best they could with what they had. As I mentioned before, my life was good. In fact, better than good. My brother and I were afforded many wonderful opportunities and most certainly had a life filled with love. My story of adoption differs in several ways, yet some of the effects on adopted children are the same. Some may think that I had it easy because I wasn't in the foster care system for very long, and I do not negate the fact that I've heard some horrible stories. In telling my story, I in no way make light of anything that any child has endured. This book is my release and a part of the legacy that I will leave my son and daughter. It is also articulated with the hope of bridging generational divides across the world.

The Moment of Truth

One evening, my family and I sat in the living room talking and everyone was discussing who they looked like on their mother's side of the family. Questions such as what attributes and characteristics they shared came up. Suddenly, my son turned towards me, and asked, "Daddy, who do we look like on your side of the family?" For the first time, I was not able to give an honest, bona fide answer. I was silent and thought to myself, "I don't know." I smiled and continued to laugh with my family, but inside my mind was swirling with questions. I began wondering, what diseases run in my family? Are there any mental illnesses? What habits and behaviors did I innately inherit? Are my habits inherited from my biological parents or learned behaviors from those I grew up around?

I realized that I didn't know anything about my bloodline. As the rest of the family continued talking, the conversation seemed a blur. I stared into space and finally decided to find the answers to my son's questions and the questions that I had asked myself for many years. I did not know where to start, so I went to the only source I knew: my adoptive mother. The only mother I'd ever known. She was mom in every sense of the word, therefore, referring to her as my adoptive mom again, is only to differentiate between the two for this book's sake. I knew that she would be 100% honest with me and support me in my quest to find my family. I was cautious with my approach because I never wanted her to ever feel that I did not love her or would place anyone else above her.

One morning, after some of my mother's world-famous pancakes (according to my stomach), I asked her about my adoption. I hadn't forgotten, I just didn't mention it for several years. I felt that the possibility of ever meeting my other family was so far-fetched that it was no sense in going backward. However, my son's question and lack of knowledge would not allow me just to brush it off as if it didn't exist.

My mother was very calm as usual, she sat at the table, put some butter and syrup on her pancakes and began to tell me what she knew about my adoption and my biological parents. She didn't withhold any information, but she also did not hide her feelings. As I spoke with her, she told me to remain cautious and to seek support from her concerning whatever I needed.

She was very protective of me and wanted to be sure that whatever the outcome of my search, I'd still be fine. It turns out, as usual, she was right. I had no idea of the journey I was about to undertake. My mother was very faithful and trustworthy and the only person that I could turn to for comfort and honest answers.

It's Time

My mom went to the safe and pulled out the same paperwork I'd stumbled upon 42 years earlier. Once I held the document of my birth in my hands, the nostalgia of my first encounter with it came rushing back. The paper still had the same feel that I remembered as I tried to make sense of the information it contained when I was a child. It was the only document that my parents had that proved my adoption, therefore, she asked me to handle it with care and to keep it in a safe place.

When I read it, I saw the attorney's information and the law firm that handled my adoption. It ended up being a friend of my adopted mom's from high school. She was the one who handled the beginning of my adoption for them. As I glared at the paper in silence, my mom encouraged me. She also gave me her blessings and guidance. I went to sit on the front porch as I still do to this day and just looked off into the distance with mixed emotions. I thought to myself, *finally, wow, you're really gonna do this*. I copied the attorney's information down on a separate piece of paper, so that the original document remained intact. I called and left messages and even spoke to a few people, but they could not point me in the right direction. It was revealed that the law firm that handled my adoption in the beginning was no longer in business.

My next option was to get the phone book and contact every Thornton listed on the page. There were not many in the listing, so I thought it would be easy to locate someone who knew me. I called and left messages with minor details of who I was. I got in contact with one lady who sounded very curious, but also very reluctant to share any of the information that I requested. However, she did tell me that she would call around and ask the people that she knew if they had any information. Days went by and she called me a few times stating that she had not heard anything, but she would keep me posted. I was very optimistic and believed that I would get some news. She told me that if I had not heard from her in a week to give her a call.

A week went by and I decided to call her. I was not able to speak to her, so I left a message. I waited several more days and tried to call again. I left several more messages, but my calls were not returned. This was the start of my anxiety and moments of doubt. I wondered if I should just dismiss the idea or persist in finding my birth parents. Thoughts plagued my mind. I wondered if the reason that she wasn't responding was because she was withholding some information. What was she hiding and what did she know? Did she contact my mother or father and they did not want to meet me? The perplexing thoughts were overwhelming. I felt an extreme amount of anxiety. Therefore, I decided that maybe I should slow the process down for the sake of my own mental health. I was creating things in my head that hadn't even happened. So, I took a few weeks off to figure out another plan. Shortly thereafter, one of the attorneys that I called finally reached back out to me and told me to check with the State Department of Health. He said that they should be able to give me some information.

The State Department of Health sent a letter giving me what they call the "unidentified" information. This information contained the ages of both of my biological parents, places of birth, hospitals, years and dates, with no names, or addresses. This was a small victory and at least I had a starting point. I noticed their ages and started to put a time frame on how long they might have left to live. Therefore, I felt that it was a race for time to find them.

Before I began my search, the following poetic words poured from my soul:

Where are you?

My first 8 months are just a blur,
I really don't have any memory
of her.
No smile, no touch, no breath,
no grin.
I can't even remember
touching her skin.
Nothing of my biologicals
is locked in my mind,
Up until year one,
I can't rewind.
Right up until the 3rd grade,
I believed I was from them,
I favored her,
last name was of him.
I accidentally found out
that I was adopted
and from that day forward,
questions played in my head.

Sitting in class
wondering who I was

Could the person next to me
be a sibling or a cuz?

Thinking that every boy that
shared my same complexion
and gap in their teeth,
could possibly be my brother.

Deep down in my heart,
I wondered about my father
and my mother.

Where are you?

I remember praying
that God would let me find you
somewhere along this race.
God please don't take them away
from this earth
until I see their face
I was 7 when I prayed
that prayer.

The thoughts that went thru
my mind as a kid,
Why did you give me up,
was it something that I did?

Would I have been an extra bill?
Was this decision made against
my father's will?

Where is he,
better yet where are you?
I heard that I had other siblings.

and that we all shared
the same DNA,

I have a question,
before you gave me up,

did you try to figure out another way?
I mean were there any other options,
any other choices,
or were you hearing the voices telling you
that this was what was best choice?

Where are you?

I don't want you to think
that I am complaining,
or I have some deep seeded issues,
because the reality is
that the other option
could have left me aborted,
contorted and distorted,
being pulled from your womb
twisted in a bloody mess,
no pieces left for a tomb.

I am looking for you,
Have you been looking for me,
or will I find out that my search was not
reciprocated?

I need to find you because I need to find me.
Who do I look like?
Whose characteristics do I share?

Does my father
have the same kinks in his hair?

I often sit back, and wonder if I'd be
where I am today If I was still there?
Who has my eyes, who has my nose?

Do you have the same
alignment in your toes?
I ask these questions because,
I got a son and he is 12, and
his origins start and end with me.

He once asked me
who he favored;
all I could say was me.
He asked who I favored;
the answer never made it past me,

That's when I realized
that all we had was we.
You see me and him are all we got,
he is the only one that I can tie to me,
that is why we are so close.

From a bloodline standpoint
its us against the world.
You would be happy to know that,
I'm educated,
employed and black,
Haven't had to kick any habits,
no monkeys on my back.

I served my country; I was a heel of a jock.
And I don't have any kids out of wedlock.
My parents put me thru the best of schools,

They always made sure I didn't grow
up with the best of fools.

What I found out
was that with all my accolades
and accomplishments,
there was still something missing.
A void of my very existence
that continued to ponder the rhetorical
question of who am I?

We may never meet,
I may never hear your voice,
There may never be a time
for our families to greet,
And I will have to deal
with your choice.

But before I close my eyes,
I hope I get the chance to see
where it all started
And maybe hear the stories
as to why we parted.

No rush, I have waited this long,
Shed my tears and sang my songs
And if this union never happens
I will find myself content,
Because the best thing
that you could have ever done
was give me up for a better life.

But.......
Where are you?

Reggie

As you can see a lot of emotions ran through my mind in penning that poem. I realized trying to get more than the identified information from the state was going to take more resilience and time. I was told that all adoptions before 1975 were closed, and everything after 1975 was open. Since I was born in 1972, my adoption was one that was sealed. This meant that the records of the biological parents of infants who were adopted during those years were kept sealed by the courts. This was to ensure that all information remained confidential. The sealed records presented another huge obstacle in my locating them. Furthermore, the unsealing would only be possible if approval in writing was granted by several of those in authority, including the attorney general and a judge.

I tried researching on my own. I found many organizations had very high fees with little to no guarantee that my biological parents would be found. I was quoted between $3000 and $5,500 with no guarantee, and that didn't sit right with me. The discouragement and fear seemed overwhelming. The voices in my head shouted, "Give it up, they don't want to see you anyway. You've had a good life, and there is no sense in walking into anything blind and not knowing if it will satisfy you!"

A short time later, someone broke into my car and stole many things, including the envelope used to store the information that I'd gathered concerning my adoption. I succumbed to the discouragement, ended my search and went back to my normal everyday life. Five years passed before I decided to pursue that endeavor again. Within that five-year time span, I went through some life-altering transitions; it seemed as though everything I'd worked to build was slowly deteriorating.

My life seemed to be going backward instead of progressing forward like I had hoped. Amid the turmoil, I needed something to keep me from crumbling. I needed to focus on something positive. I was already at a low and surmised that things could not get any worse, therefore; I decided to begin the search to find my biological parents again. This time around, I was able to find a liaison who worked within the courts, and was willing to take my case. Her fee was affordable, and the process was not as arduous of a task as those I'd contacted previously. Her name was Chris. She was very welcoming and understanding. I wasn't just another case to her. She really desired to help me. However, as much as she wanted to help, she did inform me that there could be a chance that my biological parents may not want to be contacted. She advised me to prepare myself for that possibility.

As months went by, and just when it appeared that I was getting close to finding out the information on my biological parents, the election year approached. Election time meant that our county judges could shift seats. There was a chance my case would be appointed to a new judge. Having a new judge would start the process of obtaining signatures of approval all over again and could send me back to square one with my search. Unfortunately, that ended up being the case. Another judge did get appointed, and my case was resubmitted for the appropriate signatures.

Although this set the process back a few months, I did not give up. In early May, I received a call from Chis. She told me that all of the necessary paperwork was approved, and she was able obtain my biological mother's information. However, she mentioned that the information could not be released to me, until she had the approval from my biological mother. So once again, the anxiety and fear kicked in. The defeating thoughts came rushing back to my mind. What if she says no? What if she does not want to meet or even talk to me? What if she said thanks but no thanks?

These different scenarios played back and forth in my head. I had many sleepless nights, tossing and turning, wondering, could this be it? I wondered how my story would end, and if I was setting myself up for failure? Weeks passed before I heard from Chris again. Finally, on May 21, 2014, I was given the green light to call my biological mother. I could not believe it! Finally, the answer to my prayers had arrived. I couldn't wait to hear her voice.

On my way home, I prepared what I was going to say and how I would introduce myself. But what could I possibly say to a woman that I've never met? For decades, I wondered about her voice and her laugh. Nervously, I grabbed my phone and headed to the living room so that I could gather myself and relax. I began to sweat as I felt my breath rapidly escaping from my lungs. I finally dialed the number; It seemed as if the phone rang a hundred times, but in reality it was only rang three times. I heard her say hello, and for some reason, it clicked; she sounded exactly how I thought she would sound. The pitch and tone in her voice was as if she had been talking to me every day. When you think about it, that's how it should have sounded, because I was in her stomach for nine months. I heard every word she uttered during her pregnancy with me. It laid dormant in my subconscious mind for 42 years. It's amazing how the mind works and what it can lock away until it's needed.

We were both very emotional but grateful for the amazing opportunity to reconnect with each other after all these years. In between attempting to talk and get acquainted, we both shed tears. I had so many questions swirling around in my head, but I didn't feel the time was right for me to bombard her with them. Instead, we just spent time trying to embrace the moment. Elated, humbled, and grateful, I felt that I was embarking upon a new chapter of my life.

BEYOND BLOOD 39

Chapter Four
Parental Responsibility

Parents who try to shield their children from the news of adoption do a great disservice by not giving them the opportunity to ask the necessary questions. They aren't given the chance to deal with the emotional trauma early, nor prevent the shame that may come as a result of someone else revealing the truth. Being honest also keeps the family line of communication open without the fear of betrayal and distrust.

My adoptive parents had the idea that I'd be ready to process the concept of adoption around the age of ten or eleven. I'm not sure if they were prepared when I found the paper in the safe when I was seven. But they came forward with the truth. Of course, I was too young to process it and articulate the proper questions; none-the-less, them revealing the truth was better than covering the information with a lie. And they didn't have to deal with the pain of having to re-establish trust broken by deceit.

I feel parents do more harm than good when they conceal the truth. I understand they are trying to protect the child, but they need to know the truth about who they are and where they came from. It's a roll of the dice, and the outcome could prove positive or negative, but regardless, they need to know.

I feel that the truth should be determined by the parent(s) based on the child's maturity. In my opinion, a child being told in their teenage years is too late. In their adolescent years, they are learning more about their surroundings, what social groups they belong to, or trying to fit in. They are learning about their bodies, hormones are all over the place, and they are trying to be accepted in a changing world.

From teenaged to young adult years, they are dealing with the pressures of school, athletics, college or future career choices, and or navigating thoughts of being on their own. Add to that, family, friends, and personal life. Can you imagine dropping the news of adoption on them and letting them know that everything they have come to know, and love has been a lie?

My example sums it up. I lost my (adoptive) father in my sophomore year of high school. I was angry with the world. Everything I knew was wrapped and tied up in my father's existence. He was my superhero...my man of steel. Not having him around was catastrophic on numerous levels. I played sports because of him and longed for his acceptance and validation. Within a matter of months, I watched him deteriorate in front of my eyes, and it was devastating. As a result, I had a "me against the world" mentality.

Can you imagine being told you're adopted at the most critical time in your life? There is a chance that information could cripple a child and possibly set them back. I'm grateful that I knew early on, and although I still had to walk through my share of pain, it wasn't as severe as it could have been.

As parents, it's imperative to identify when the time is right. Remember how important your emotional support is to the adopted child. And never be so insecure that you try to prevent the child from learning about his/her biological family. Even if they decide the pursuit of knowing is too daunting of a task at the time, there is a chance that they could change their minds later in life. When they do, support is always better than personal feelings or biases.

I mentioned in the beginning that my story is a lot different. Some of my friends have found out news concerning adoption later in life. Because I was very young when I found out, it didn't hit me the same. Maybe because I was too young to fully process it, therefore, I wasn't blown away by the news. It didn't come as a shock. Honestly, I didn't know how to feel. I just continued enjoying being a kid. And although the initial news wasn't the same for me as it was for some, I did eventually go through an identity crisis. I believe the longer parents wait, the more damage will be done in the future. I've done ample research on this subject, spoken with others who found out they were adopted, and my own personal experience taught me that each individual will process the information differently. Therefore, as they cycle through the series of emotions and maybe even question adoptive parents, one common question is going to be "Why?" Most want to know why the biological parents elected not to fulfill the responsibility of raising and nurturing them. This is where the adoptive parent's support, validation, and affirmation will provide emotional healing.

Without it, a cycle of seeking affirmation from the wrong sources could easily develop. I want to list several reasons why concealing the truth about adoption is negative. Not telling a child can lead to feelings of betrayal, loss of trust, and an identity crisis later in life. Keeping adoption a secret can create a culture of shame and secrecy and prevent the child from feeling accepted and loved for who they are. Not knowing their biological family history can put the child at risk for certain medical conditions that may be genetic. Additionally, not telling a child they are adopted can lead to missed opportunities for support and resources. I will always be thankful for the way my parents handled conveying such sensitive information. I am also grateful that it allowed me to have a choice and a voice as I became an adult. I am forever grateful.

It is a good idea to tell a child they are adopted for several reasons. Firstly, it promotes honesty and trust between parents and children. Secondly, it helps children develop a sense of identity, which is crucial for their mental and emotional development. Thirdly, it normalizes adoption and reduces stigma, promoting inclusivity. Fourthly, it prevents shock and trauma when children discover the truth later in life.

Finally, it helps children access important medical information by knowing their biological family history, which can lead to preventative measures and early interventions. Overall, being open and honest with the child from an early age about their adoption status is essential for their emotional, mental, and physical well-being. In such instances, the primary goal for parents is to maintain the child's trust and confidence when revealing their adoption status. Children look to their parents for honesty and openness, particularly during crucial developmental phases. Delaying this information may lead children to question themselves and feel uncertain. They will inevitably seek answers and harbor fears, but providing reassurance will help them comprehend the situation better.

Children sometimes grow up with daddy and mommy issues. Even more so, for many who are adopted. Birth parents also deal with the never-ending guilt of giving the child up for adoption. Closed adoptions and the lies associated with them, can leave them wondering if their children are doing okay, or if they will ever be reconnected to them. Most will conceal these birth facts as their new lives progress, even birthing other children. When the adopted child learns of their birth parents, they will have to deal with wondering if the birth parents ever looked for them. Some will even conclude, if they were able to find the birth parent, why couldn't the birth parent find them? Moreover, the pain of thinking that other children may have been kept will contribute to the emotional complexities. The journey of reconnecting with one's biological family can be an emotional roller coaster filled with anticipation, uncertainty, and hope. Personally, I had reservations prior to meeting my biological family. I endured sleepless nights wondering if I'd be accepted and if we'd have the happy ending that my heart desired. I've come to understand that the same emotional turmoil is a shared experience among adoptees. It is evident that the emotional toll of discovering one's biological family remains difficult, regardless of the timing of the reunion. Adoptees who are ready to find hope in their situation can locate support groups that aid them in bonding over their shared apprehensions and uncertainties. There is comfort in knowing others have walked similar paths. These sacred spaces create a supportive community that dispels feelings of isolation and misunderstanding. While each reunion is unique, adoptees universally face emotional challenges that require courage to navigate. Embracing these emotions paves the way for healing and establishing new connections with their biological family.

I appreciate the mutual respect that my adoptive family and my biological family have for one another. We realize the difficult, yet great experience of adoption. It gave my adoptive mom the awesome opportunity to have me. We understand that adoption was the best decision they could have made. The societal perception of adoption has evolved from a past marked by negative stigma to a present where a new, positive light is shed. This shift is pivotal in transforming adoption from a source of shame to a place of courage and strength. Parents who are unable to provide the optimal environment for their child's growth, must make the courageous choice between life and death. Embracing this positive narrative not only empowers these parents but also highlights the act of adoption as a noble decision rooted in love and selflessness. By reshaping the conversation around adoption, we pave the way for a more inclusive and compassionate society that celebrates the diverse paths to building strong and loving families.

Getting to Know Your Birth Parents

After such a stressful searching process to locate birth parents, the adrenaline rush that starts exuberant, can slowly wean away. Birth parents must remember that it is a process. Remember that time is everything. Therefore, do not expect the biological child to immediately refer to you as mom or dad. Navigating the new relationship will not be an overnight process. Therefore, take it one day at a time. Don't be upset if every call isn't answered, and you don't hear from them every day. More than likely, adopted parents are still a major part of their lives, and those are the voices they've become accustomed to hearing daily.

Although you share a significant blood connection, remember you have just reconnected. In fact, you are still strangers. Depending on the amount of time that has passed, there may be many years of information to cram into a week or a month of conversations. Patience during this process will open up a safe space for all parties. The process can't be rushed, and you should not place unfair demands on the amount of time it takes. Put yourself in the son's or daughter's shoes. They've had the most challenges with the new information. Moreover, their feelings should override yours. This isn't to invalidate your feelings, but your prioritizing them will gain their trust. Eventually, you will notice the walls coming down, and visits, conversations, and outings more routine.

If you are a parent to other children, you will also have to take the lead in being sure the child given up for adoption doesn't feel any partiality. Your home may be filled with loving photos of those children with the absent child still processing the feelings of abandonment. Allowing the siblings to slowly build and develop a bond will prove worthwhile. The relation of the birth parent and the child put up for adoption is an individualized experience for everyone; take it slow and seek a family therapist if necessary.

Reginald and mom, Norma Smith.

Chapter Five
Six Degrees Of Separation

Six degrees of separation is the theory that any person on the planet can be connected to any other person on the planet through a chain of acquaintances that has no more than five intermediaries. The concept was originally set out in a 1929 short story by Frigyes Karinthy, in which a group of people play a game of trying to connect any person in the world to themselves by a chain of five others. It was popularized in John Guare's 1990 play Six Degrees of Separation. The idea is sometimes generalized to the average social distance being logarithmic in the size of the population. In more modern terminology, we'd simply say, "small world."

I was amazed to discover that I grew up around my biological family and didn't know it. When I was in high school, I had a good friend, whose house I'd hang out at every weekend. His mother was very ill. I found out that my biological dad also knew her. Minutes apart, we'd miss one another's visits. My biological father brought her food and care packages. My friend often remarked how much I favored his mother's "friend."

It was crazy how adamant he was about how much we favored. He'd swear I had a twin. I've always heard that everyone in the world has a twin somewhere, so with that in mind, it blew right over my head. Neither of us had any idea that it was actually my biological dad who was visiting his mom. It's crazy that our paths never crossed, because literally, I'd just leave their home, and he'd come by. Or vice versa, he'd leave just before I arrived to hang out with my friend. Even more crazy, people in the same town where I grew up often asked if my dad's name was Champ? I didn't know he went by the nickname, "Champ." When people saw me, they'd automatically assume I was his son. I cannot count how many times I'd heard the name Champ growing up. I'm sure as much as people were telling me that Champ must be related to me, they were also telling him that he had a son out there or someone who resembled him so closely that they'd confuse us.

Reginald A. Smith Sr.				Homer Thornton (Champ)
									Biological Father

It still baffles me that no one ever thought to call him and say, "Stay where you are, I'm bringing someone to meet you!"

I also discovered that I used to play baseball a block away from where my biological aunts grew up. It is a strong possibility that I played with them or hung out with them and didn't know we were related. I also found out that a lot of my friends shared friendships with several people in my biological family. Talk about six degrees of separation! We were all connected in some way, but never imagined that we were biologically related. I guess at the time, no one's focus was on the fact that I was adopted. We simply went along with life.

After graduating high school, my best friend and I liked older women. I know we were crazy, but we often snuck into nightclubs. I remember women thinking my name was Champ or would say something like, "Champ must have a son that he doesn't know about."

We frequented the same nightclubs and hung around the same people. How uncanny is that? My biological father and I were almost identical. We were the same height and build. They could hardly believe that I didn't know him and was not his son. Again, he and I missed one another by seconds or minutes.

One lady said to me one night, "You just left and came back already?" She mistook me for him. If anyone had mentioned a last name, I would have known instantly that it was my biological father. But all they'd say was Champ. Our resemblance was so strong that at times, people would really examine me. They'd look me up and down in sheer amazement.

After talking to my biological family, I also discovered that my biological father lived several blocks down from me as an adult. I lived at 3902 Hemlock. My biological mother told me that my dad lived on 35th and Hemlock. It's still mind-blowing that we have never bumped into one another or met face to face.

Six degrees of separation proves to be more than just a theory.

My adoptive mother told me she wanted me to find my family, she was supportive but wanted to remain at a distance. Again, I want to reiterate that I am separating them by adoptive and biological for clarity in sharing my story. Adoptive in no way indicates that she isn't my actual mother. She's incredible. I could not have asked for a better family. My "adoptive" parents were hard-working and loving. They made sure that all of my needs, wants, and desires were met. And our home was never void of love. Therefore, meeting my additional family gave me the best of both worlds.

I remember praying that God would allow me to meet my biological parents before they passed away. Age and timing in my mind, was always a factor. Unfortunately, I missed my biological father by several months. He passed away before we could meet. I used to wonder if he and I would have reconciled if I had not put off re-opening the records of the sealed adoption. I'd become burdened with the process and put it on hold for five years.

But that is a weight that is too heavy to carry. I had to learn to release myself from the guilt because God who is Omniscient, knew long before I did, that meeting him would not happen. I still find joy in tracing my roots and discovering the wonder of being his son. His DNA is evident from the facial features, body stature, and mannerisms.

As I reflect, I guess I was spared from having to face the physical loss of two dads, since my wonderful adoptive father was also deceased. Regret and guilt both have negative effects on emotions. I learned to recognize and validate my feelings, so that they do not unconsciously, and subconsciously affect my future relationships and decisions.

We've all heard, "Never put off for tomorrow, what you can

do today." Unfortunately, that lesson is easier to learn when you realize that time is a precious commodity; when it's gone, you can never get it back. Self-forgiveness helps us to realize that we are simply human. Most times, we do the best with what we have in the moment. It sounds cliche' but without the space to make mistakes, we'd put more demands upon ourselves than necessary. That is a demon I'm all too familiar with.

Remember, I battled with always having to prove my worth. I'm overcoming it little by little. As I learn the lessons from my regrets in life, I pray that you also will find the courage to move forward and choose wiser. T.D. Jakes wrote in his book *Maximize the Moment* that we must seize every opportunity that we are given. He said that life is too short to allow yourself to be an inmate in a prison of bad choices and weak decisions. The prison of previous mistakes comes with jailers of guilt and regret. Together, they hold you captive, torturing you with images of what you should have done and what you could have accomplished. Most of us don't realize that the key to releasing ourselves is within our own hands.

The words Pastor Jakes wrote are very profound and wise. I've learned that torturing ourselves with feelings of lost or failed opportunities robs us of life's most precious moments. Bitterness is debilitating and will leave us living beneath our best selves. Therefore, we would be incapable of giving our family and friends the joy of living with us in a pleasant and peaceful environment.

Going back to the movie that captivated my heart, *Antwoine Fisher*. It took me on an emotional roller coaster as his story paralleled mine in many ways. After some time, Antwoine was able to locate his biological family. Although our feet didn't travel the exact same path, my desire to know and connect with my biological family and the hope for acceptance was synonymous with his. Towards the end of the movie, I was an emotional wreck! Especially during the scene where he walked into his aunt's house and was finally introduced to many of his family members.

As the scene progressed, they opened doors that led to a large dining room. The elders of the family were seated at a formal dining room table. The feast that was prepared in his honor showed how thrilled they were to have him home. It was very heartwarming. One woman, who appeared to be the great-grandmother, knocked on the table and motioned for him to come close to her. She gazed up with tears in her eyes as she gently touched his face. She gracefully said, "Welcome." By this time, half the Kleenex in the box I held was gone. My heart was overwhelmed as my soul ached for such a reunion with my own biological family.

After the initial conversation with my biological mom, I finally got the chance to have the family reunion I've always wanted. It was May 2014. Seven days before her birthday. I was 42 years old at the time. My son and I drove down to Cincinnati, Ohio to meet her and a few of my cousins. She embraced me and couldn't stop hugging me. In the evening, she told me that she even peeked into the room as I slept. She said she'd always hoped that I was alive and well. She'd never forgotten about me. She also wondered if I favored her or my father. Throughout my visit, she constantly showered me with affection through gentle touches and embraces.

Since that meeting, we talked on the phone at least three days a week. Listening to her, even at her age, I could tell that she was super intelligent. My biological mother shared some of her family's history with me. I found out that she really endured a lot growing up. She told me that her father was deceased, and her mother died by suicide. It was tragic to hear how they found her body on the street. She had already given birth to my older brother by the time she found out that I was growing inside of her womb. She told me that his father and her didn't work out.

When she spoke about my father, she couldn't recall all that happened between them, but her environment and the toxicity of her family took a toll on her mental well-being. She felt that my brother and I deserved more than she could offer either of us at the time.

Life hit her hard and she spiraled downward. Instead of aborting me, she decided adoption would be best. She sent my older brother to live with my aunt and tried to dig herself out of the pit she was in. She told me that my biological father was a Vietnam veteran and suffered some issues as a result. With both of them fighting to survive emotionally and mentally, they never had a solid relationship.

It is difficult to put into words what hearing these stories for the first time did to me emotionally. However, I am grateful that they were wise enough to allow a loving family to raise me. And because of the standards they set, I was able to be a productive and successful man. I had my flaws, as you've read, but without the foundation that I had growing up, there is no doubt that I would have probably gone through much worse. As difficult as these things were to hear, it's funny how life works out just as God orchestrates it.

My Family

My biological mother had three other children. And my biological dad had a daughter. So that is four additional siblings. They all knew about me and stated that they tried to find me, but their efforts were unsuccessful. Ironically, I lived in Indiana at the time and lived on 56th and Post Road. My niece told me that one of my sisters lived 15 minutes from me at that same time. Here we are at six degrees of separation again. Unfortunately, she died from a brain aneurysm, so I did not get a chance to meet her. However, I did meet her children, my niece, and nephew.

When I was finally united with my brothers, we shared a lot of past photos and cried as we embraced one another. Seeing my family was mind blowing. I felt like I was on the red carpet. They were all stunned and stared at me. The moment was surreal, and partially uncomfortable as I was the center of attention. I felt a little naked and exposed. I think they were captivated by me being the exact replica of my biological dad. His height, build, cadence, the way he moved when he walked, and other mannerisms.

The embrace and excitement from my aunt who kept hugging me and crying, made me feel like a kid again. That little boy who struggled with his identity, felt some sort of relief. Again, I couldn't quite grasp the feelings of consolation, because like I stated before, my family was great. I never felt any sense of loss until my adoptive father passed away.

Psychologically, it goes back to what took place over me spiritually in the womb. I had no idea the effect it would have on me until much later in life.

My aunt's embrace was so warm and loving, she looked at me and exclaimed, "What! Where did you come from?"

She could hardly believe her eyes. She was so excited and humble. Her embrace made me feel safe; I melted into her arms because her touch was healing to my soul. We spent the rest of the evening talking and getting acquainted.

Overall, their acceptance was great. It was wonderful meeting everyone and I have no regrets reuniting with any of them. My mother said, every year around my birthday, she'd fall into depression and wonder if I was alive and how I was doing. My brothers told me that reuniting with me brought joy and peace into their lives.

When I first met my biological mother, she told me throughout the years, she feared that I would carry bitterness and resentment towards her for giving me up for adoption. I immediately told her that I did not have any bitterness towards her. I have worked in the system for over two decades and I have had the opportunity to witness homes torn apart by bitterness and unforgiveness. But for me, I was blessed not to experience any of that because of the loving family who adopted me. I reassured my mother that there was no bitterness. However, I did mention, if I had experienced any of the traumas outlined in the film *Antoine Fisher*, or if I had faced any abuse or extreme neglect, my response may have been different.

Depending on the severity of the trauma, healing can be quite a journey. Gratefully, my story makes me think of Moses in the Bible. His mother was not allowed to raise him in his present environment and the conditions were not suitable for him to thrive or survive. Being selfish and trying to keep him in a stressful environment would not have allowed him to operate in his purpose and fulfill his destiny; in fact his demise would have been imminent.

She wanted a better life for him. One that was filled with love, fulfillment, and prosperity. Had she not given him up, he wouldn't have risen through the ranks as he did in Egypt as a prince, and a highly esteemed military leader. Eventually Moses became the deliverer for the children of Israel. He is listed among those hailed as great heroes of the faith. In a nutshell he would have never been the man he was destined to become.

This goes for me as well, had I stayed in the environment of my birth, there would have been a strong chance, the person I am today may not have come to fruition. I'm not making myself out to be Moses, but when I review his story, I can see a reason biblically for the adoption. His mother was able to spare his life through giving him up. I was able to thrive, prosper and be around people who could positively impact my life.

I am not stating that all of my relatives had a bad upbringing, this is my assessment, based on what my biological mother conveyed about her own life's experience and the turmoil that she was in. Because of her unselfish decision, I was allotted the opportunity to attend the best schools, travel, and be exposed to great things at an early age. I told her I was grateful for what she did. I understood that it wasn't because she didn't love me, but that she loved me enough to possibly give me a chance at more than she could offer at the time.

Who could be mad at that? The more I ponder the life of Moses, his life came full circle as he was nursed by the mother who gave him up. Just as he brought deliverance to Israel, the joy and peace that God gave my family through our connection was able to bring deliverance from pain, guilt, and depression. One final thought on this analogy is, once pain heals, clarity comes and obscurity fades. The wounds that were trapped behind unanswered questions from my youth, were slowly healed with each encounter with my family.

On my biological father's side, I finally got the reassurance that his family did think of me and even attempted to find me. That answered life-long questions that plagued me when I began my own search. I don't know when they found out about me, but I do know that it wasn't until later in life.

The stories around my mother's pregnancy seem conflicting. I saw videos and photos of her pregnant surrounded by her family. It seems strange that no one put 2&2 together or asked what happened to her baby. It's confusing to me because she didn't vanish or go into hiding for the nine months of her pregancy. She was alive and in living color. However, I'm still grateful that even after years passed, once they found out, they longed to know me.

Additionally, I was finally able to get a lot of questions about my personality answered. How uncanny is it that my dad and I both went into the military? I love archery, and I was told that he loved it and also taught archery classes. I have a passion for hunting. He also loved the sport of hunting. My heart smiles when I think of how alike we really were.

From left to right, little brother, Renarde, and me, Reggie.

Chapter Six
My Brother's Keeper

When I returned home, my brother from my adoptive parents (Renarde) and I had a much-needed conversation. He and I never discussed my adoption. I'm the oldest, yet he is very protective of me. After my 50th birthday, we decided to sit and talk. It was the first time that he'd ever asked about my adoption. I never brought it up to him because I didn't want him to feel that he'd be replaced by my biological brothers.

He initiated the conversation, which brought me great comfort. Having his support meant everything to me. I was able to be open and transparently disclose my most intimate thoughts. It felt good to share with him the details of finding and meeting my biological family. I was afraid that he'd feel abandoned by me and that is why I never talked to him about it. It goes back to the fear of rejection and not wanting others to be upset.

Not being able to share one of the most vital pieces of completeness and closure in my life felt like a huge weight. A heaviness that I carried because of my own fears. I do not regret considering his or anyone else's feelings, because being empathetic is a part of my nature. However, I did have to learn how to balance caring about others, without sacrificing my own wholeness. I haven't fully mastered it; thus, it is still a part of my therapy. At its root, it's still an attempt to avoid rejection.

Truthfully, no one really knows how they will respond until they are faced with certain situations, but as we mature, we must all learn to deal with life as it comes with positive attitudes and behaviors. It's a part of growth. Despite our three-year age difference, Renarde and I have always been close. We did everything together growing up and although he is the baby, my parents never showed any partiality. Because of the values that they instilled within us regarding family, we grew up with love and trust.

From what I've seen personally in many homes, a lot of family breakdowns happen because the matriarchs fail to set the standard and establish the foundation of "family first." We were blessed to have parents that did. As a result, he became my confidant, best friend, and everything you can imagine a brother being. We share the same moral character and zest for life. We currently live in different states, but we talk four to five times a week. It is because of the mutual respect and honor that we have for one another, that nothing can separate or break the bond that we have.

During the month of January in 2022, 10 months before my birthday, I began planning a huge celebration. I was turning the big 50, so I was planning to do it big! I wanted to be surrounded by my friends and family, which also included uniting my brother Renarde and my biological brothers. Six months into the planning, I began to experience various bouts of anxiety and I could not pinpoint its origin. Then it hit me…suddenly a rush of emotion swelled over me as I thought to myself, "my brothers (biological and the only brother I'd ever known) have never met one another." There I was, once again overcome with fear. I wondered how they would respond to one another and how my relationship with each of them might change. Plus, I thought of all the relatives on my (adoptive) parents' side of the family who knew Renarde as my only brother. The majority of them had no idea that I was adopted and had other siblings.

The anxiety hit me so hard that I debated about having a small celebration rather than inviting everyone and dealing with their reactions. My true fear was finally releasing the secret that I'd kept for so long. Only one cousin in my adoptive family knew of my adoption and like I mentioned earlier in this book, he has never told a soul. I allowed panic to come in because I wasn't sure how it would all turn out.

However, I'm glad that I didn't allow fear to make the decision on whether to change my plans or cancel them. I didn't allow my own negative perceptions of how I thought other people would feel, react, or respond to influence me. The weird thing about fear is it doesn't give us the opportunity to check facts; it simply attempts to control outcomes. And it will rob us of opportunities, connections, and blessings, if we allow it to keep us from taking risks.

The path that God carved out for me was never a mistake. It was all in His beautifully laid plan. My role amid the detours was to find hope, purpose, and fulfilment. Like a carefully orchestrated puzzle, all the pieces were fitting together. Fear was losing its grip over me. I'm slowly conquering it and reclaiming my power to live without emotional limits.

When my birthday finally arrived on November 3, I was grateful to be alive. I'd overcome so much already and reflected on those who did not make it to see 50 years of age. I was completely humbled. I finally resolved that my birthday would be special, and the meeting would work how God intended. My wife knew of my previous struggle with planning my party and asked how I felt about my family meeting for the first time? I replied, "It is what it is, and what shall be, shall be."

The Meeting/ My Birthday Celebration

We each lived in different states, so my biological brothers and I had only gotten together a few times. This meeting was going to be monumental. The excitement and intensity grew as each of them arrived one by one. The kickoff celebration party was going to be held at a restaurant called BJ's.

My wife and I arrived with other family members as we all celebrated. My biological brothers Todd and Donny came through the door, and we greeted one another with hugs and slight punches in the side. I was honored to introduce my children to their uncles and the rest of my wife's side of the family. (That was the easy part). But it was my side of the family on my adoptive parent's side that had me more concerned. Todd is the eldest of the four biological brothers. I'm the second oldest, third is Donny and Johnathan is the baby boy on my mom's side of the family. From what I was told about them, Todd became "caregiver" and "protector" of his younger siblings, Donny and Johnathan. He and Donny are about 10 years apart. Once he grew up and went into the military, they were responsible for themselves. Yet they have an incredible bond as well. Because of Johnathan's health concerns, he couldn't attend the celebration. However, he and I have spoken and I am just as eager to meet him in person. He is in my heart.

At the party, my brother Renarde finally hit the scene about a half-hour later and we greeted one another the same way we've done since we were kids. I took a deep breath and said to myself, "okay, it's showtime!" I introduced Todd and Donny to Renarde. We chatted, danced, ate, and had a great time. Surprisingly, Renarde, Todd, and Donny greeted one another with such synergy, you'd think we were all raised in the same household or that they'd known one another all their lives. The transition was smooth. Everyone bonded and it was instantaneous. It wasn't something that took a long while and I'm grateful. Everyone has a process and I understand that. I'm just grateful that mine has taken a turn for the better. God has truly been gracious to me in this. Growing up with my brother Renarde was the best blessing in the world. To add to that, God gave me more. We are more than siblings, I have lifelong allies, who will forever have my back and I theirs. This bond of brotherhood gives us safe spaces to grow and build while enjoying companionship, protection, playful teasing, and friendly competition. Did I mention the endless laughter? Yes, my brothers are truly special.

Part two of my celebration was to be a family dinner. That is where I planned to announce my adoption and my biological family to my adoptive family. When that time came and I was expressing my appreciation for all who were in attendance and all those who were near and dear to my heart, I decided to let the cat out of the bag. As I stood talking, my heart felt like it was going to jump out of my chest. It was beating faster than a trained drummer. I finally mustered up the courage and spilled the beans about my adoption.

I introduced my biological brothers to everyone. I glanced over the room and saw the amazement on their faces. I saw eyebrows arch and jaws drop in awe. But there was still a sense of freedom and joy that came over me. It was just like when I was seven and I first told my friends about my adoption. After the initial shock, they all went back to being kids, playing and doing normal kid stuff, like I had not said a thing. Well, the exact same thing happened.

After the announcement, everyone resumed the normal celebration. They were eating and laughing as if we were those same kids from the second grade. To see my family and friends embrace my brothers, and laugh and crack jokes with one another made my heart cry with joy. I'd never been happier.

I've heard that men enjoy activities together but do not know how to dwell together in unity, deep conversation, worship, and understanding. Add to that the "sharing of tears." That sounds horrible to say. A part of me shudders; one, because it's hard to imagine men tearing up over everything, and two, because we've been repeatedly told that "men don't cry!" But if we are honest, life can offer us a plethora of things that hurt and wound us. Especially, the death of a parent, spouse, or child. Just look around at the people in the room when Lance, played by Morris Chestnut, lost his wife Mia, played by Monica Calhoun, in *The Best Man Holiday*. In the heart-wrenching funeral scene, Lance, played by Morris Chestnut, experiences an immense loss as he bids farewell to his beloved wife.

As the funeral reaches its poignant finale, Lance's grief becomes palpable, evident in the tear-stained faces of those surrounding him. With each person in attendance representing a unique connection to Lance and Mia's life together, the room is filled with a mix of sorrow and support. Friends, family, and loved ones all gather to pay their respects, their eyes reflecting both empathy and shared pain, as Quentin, portrayed by Terrance Howard, finds it difficult to contain the painful loss. The intensity of his pain is shown by his deep soul cries and the profuse amount of tears. It is in this moment that the power of emotion takes center stage.

The scene moves to the cemetery, still echoing the voice of Harper, played by Taye Diggs, as he gives the heart-wrenching eulogy. Lance stands beside the casket; the weight of his loss becomes too much to bear. His shoulders slump, his hands tremble, and his anguish reverberates through the entire moment. The camera captures every raw and vulnerable expression etched across his face, showcasing a depth of sorrow that words alone cannot convey.

Harper keenly senses the breaking point of his dear friend. In a swift movement, he rushes to Lance's side, his own heart heavy with sorrow and empathy. As the casket is slowly lowered into the ground, the finality of the moment hits Lance with a crushing force. Unable to stand under the weight of his grief any longer, Lance collapses to the ground, tears streaming down his face and his words reflect the pain of letting her go. Harper, ever loyal and compassionate, catches him, and embraces him in his arms offering both physical and emotional support. In this powerful display of friendship, we witness the true essence of vulnerability and brokenness.

This scene resonates deeply with all viewers, stirring a myriad of emotions within. It reminds us of the fragility of life and the profound impact that loss can have on our spirits. Through the skillful performances of Morris Chestnut and Taye Diggs, the audience is transported into this world of sorrow, feeling the weight of each tear and the ache of every broken heart. *The Best Man Holiday* captures a universal truth: Grief can break even those who appear the strongest. Which often leaves us in a place where vulnerability can no longer be hidden. It is in these moments that we find the power of connection. Friends become pillars of strength, supporting one another through the darkest of times.

This scene serves further as a poignant reminder that within our shared vulnerability lies the potential for healing and resilience. Through the art of storytelling, we are invited to reflect on our own experiences of loss and the importance of compassion in times of sorrow.

Grief, at its core, is a deeply human response to the loss of someone or something significant in our lives. It is commonly associated with the death of a loved one, yet grief can extend beyond that and reflect any form of loss. e.g., the loss of a job, relationship, friendship, possessions through disaster, or other means, etc.

Whatever the loss, it is vital to be surrounded by those who love us and can help us walk through pain. Even after films such as these, some men hold on to false information and lies concerning true "masculinity." I am my brother's keeper. We are living proof that not all statistics are true.

Renarde and I have always been more than brothers, we are friends. I also love and appreciate the guy's trips my friends and I take. While I am more apt to share advice than I am to seek it from my friends, I'm learning that vulnerability has its place in our circles. I am aware that most men would rather play up masculinity, enjoy competitive sports, card games, checkers, and share a beer over jokes rather than talk about their health, wives, temptations, frustrations, and failures. However, these are the conversations needed to keep us grounded and ultimately accountable.

The Bible says there is safety in a multitude of counselors. Real friends and family won't allow you to self-destruct. But people can only help if you are honest enough to admit the need for help. I believe we are coming into an era of men realizing the need for male-to-male relationships. The stigma around being homosexual must be destroyed if we are to become the men our families need us to be. If we find it difficult to relate to other men, more than likely, we haven't found the courage to relate to ourselves and our sons.

I am grateful for mature fellowship among brethren. The wrong or immature group will most likely give the antiquated advice of finding a distraction, like having affairs, or sharing a drink or smoke. I think we can all agree these bandages are counter-productive. We cannot be a generation of men that pat one another on the back and justify improper behavior. Manhood is confronting wrong and offering viable solutions to right the wrong. Even if we do not have all the answers.

True brotherhood is providing a shoulder when needed,
being arms when strength is depleted.
Ears when listening is greater than words;
being present for the joys, celebrating the wins,
and when the lines of life seem blurred,
it is sight when vision is obscured.
I am my brother's keeper!

Brothers from left to right: Renarde Smith, Todd White, Reginald A. Smith and Donny Cundiff.

Chapter Seven
Faulty Construction

By now, you have read all about the compilation of hidden and unidentified emotional turmoil that I was in. At the age of 22, I jumped into a marriage and to be honest, I had no business marrying anyone's daughter at that age or stage in my life. We tried for many years to build a foundation, but our construction was faulty. Neither of us were mature enough to understand the true covenant of marriage. She felt safe and I now realize that although we loved one another, mutual exuberance, and attraction, isn't enough to heal a wounded soul. Honestly, we had no idea that healing was needed. We simply tried to build a marriage based on what was modeled before us.

Aside from being attractive and fun to be around, her presence represented the comfort that I needed. Instead of her love aiding in my wholeness, it became my crutch. One that I'd use and abuse. I don't mean physically, it was emotional abuse.

From 1995-2006, we unsuccessfully tried to establish an infrastructure. Although today, I can take accountability for 60% of our marital demise; But during our marriage, I'm sure she bore the brunt of the blame. Times of ignorance can really destroy a person and all other relationships connected to them. In our delusion, we see things from our own perspective. Whether right or wrong, they become the truth that justifies poor behavior. Rejection creates walls. I held strong defenses. The walls I built around protecting myself from pain usually shut everyone else out. I'd go into a dark place of isolation. It's like living with someone who occupies the same space but is distant in emotions and feelings. In a sense, it protected me, but it also wounded her. Silent treatment is a means of control through non-verbal communication. It is a tool of manipulation used to control a person or situation.

Unfortunately, that was a lesson learned a little too late. I had no idea that my shutting people out was an attempt to control them. I can picture women in my head right now practically begging me to talk to them. At other times, the silent treatment created space for negative behavior to be brushed under the rug. Most women are more adept at allowing things to slide, even if it's something as hurtful as cheating, as long as men stay or communicate again.

Without realizing it, I subjugated women into complying with me, even if it meant their own discomfort. It is also defined as passive-aggressive emotional abuse. A person who walks under the strong cloak of rejection will put unfair demands upon people who have nothing to do with their poisonous roots. They unintentionally become targets or bandages, depending on the direction the pendulum swings at the time.

When our marriage ended, I faced shame and felt devalued. Still, out of that union came two beautiful children. Our offspring deserved a complete family circle, but we found it best to divorce. As painful as it was for us, we knew they'd have to grow up with the stigma of having divorced parents. We wanted to give them the assurance that it wasn't their fault. Although we hadn't matured enough to know how our brokenness would affect them, I'm glad we've both grown. I find that redefining myself and getting the needed help will still be a benefit to them in the long run. Wholeness takes time. Life offers us a lot of fire (peaks and valleys) that purges our impurities.

Children are gifts to us. The Bible says, "Blessed is the man who has his quiver full of them." It is our responsibility to ensure that they heal from any past trauma as well. As we steward them, apologies are also necessary and will do wonders for their souls. Being transparent and letting them know that adults still deal with past trauma will help them deal with their own humanness. Failures are a part of life. And we all know they do not have to be final. I'm still learning to be open with them, even though they are young adults. It will teach them the importance of communication, so that they do not have to walk those same paths or repeat negative behaviors. As I apply words of affirmation to my own life, it is important that my children are affirmed through me. It is one thing to provide, it is another thing entirely for audible words of affirmation to fill their souls. I never want them to experience any ounce of low self-worth.

The other part of my self-preservation was to simply walk or run away. Even before my first marriage and especially after it failed, I'd end a relationship before the sting of rejection could attack my soul. I became what I feared most, the re-jec-tor. It caused me to be noncommittal. One minute I'd be all in, but the moment the fear of rejection came into play, I'd walk away. At the time, it was risk aversion. I would avoid taking the risk of remaining in a relationship where I was convinced the person would walk away from me. Therefore, rather than giving them the satisfaction of hurting me, I'd hurt them.

In addition to my personal therapy sessions, my current wife and I are also in couples counseling. I am still uncovering and dealing with the roots of rejection. Because of the purity of her love, coupled with her patience, we have decided that we must fight for our relationship. We are determined to emerge victorious in our God ordained covenant. The Bible teaches us that a threefold cord is not easily broken. We apply biblical principles, and still employ therapy to aid in healing past wounds. Both have proven effective in our healing process. She was able to confront me with the fact that I'd continued to guard my heart. I thought shutting people out was a habit, but it was deeply entrenched in my soul. It formed a part of my personality. That defense mechanism was so deeply imbedded within me that it was second nature. I discovered that it also led to my being vengeful, which also stems from rejection.

I see where this behavior has also carried over into my business relationships. It took all these years to finally hear it and acknowledge its damaging effects. Our resolve is to break negative cycles and secure marital blessings for future generations. My wife is helping me to understand that being vulnerable doesn't take away from me, it adds to the beauty and trust in our relationship. No one likes being rejected. But for me the pain went well beyond hurt feelings. It was very catastrophic. Looking back, it is very spiritual. I know in our day and time, we can over spiritualize things. Because of the bondage that held me captive, I can say for certain that it was very spiritual. It was almost as if I'd become someone I didn't even recognize.

At one time, it pushed me to drink alcohol. I was able to cut it off before it spiraled too far out of control. Yet, the other effects of rejection took control of my life. I plunged deep into promiscuity. Those women had no idea that moments of pleasure for me had nothing to do with love. They were simply used in my attempts to mask my identity crisis.

On the spiritual side also, what I internalized as being malicious from my wife, would be totally opposite of her character and nature. She is the most loving soul, and I consider myself incredibly blessed to be with a woman of her caliber.

But even in the smallest disagreement, the devil would plant thoughts in my head about her that I knew were not true. Several years ago, Joyce Meyer gave us a book that revolutionized mental assaults. *The Battlefield of the Mind* told the world how to overcome negative thoughts. Alongside the Bible, it gave us practical steps to bring our thoughts into captivity. A whole new world is opened to us when we learn to choose our thoughts instead of allowing the devil to plant his corruption into our minds. Rejection will cause a person to think of someone rejecting them, even if it's just a difference of opinion. The truth is that the enemy lies to us, so that truth remains a blur. The greater the blur, the more we will act on the lie. He plants subtle suggestions, suspicions, fears, and doubts into our minds. When we accept these negative implants from the enemy, they become what the Bible refers to as "strongholds."

It has been a fight for me to combat these negative thoughts. In the past, not being able to control my thoughts has also sent me deep into rebellion. These negative patterns have been a part of me for as long as I can remember. During my formative teen years, they came to the surface after my (adoptive) father's passing. Although it seems late, I'm glad to finally work towards healing.

The proverb, "As a person thinks in his heart, so is he," tells us how powerful our thoughts are. Our actions are direct results of our thoughts. It is a true tug-of-war between our subconscious and conscious mind. For a long time, I ignored my patterns. It's uncanny how dysfunction can become normal. Why was the enemy working overtime to be sure that I failed in my relationships and failed in my attempts to have real joy? The enemy knows the greatness on the inside of us. The Bible tells us that the enemy of our souls seeks to steal, kill, and to destroy. Keeping me in bondage would ensure that my seed would also be bound. Furthermore, he knew this book would one day come forward and it would allow men a safe place to be open and be vulnerable. It would not only convey my story of adoption, but it would serve as an apology to the women I wounded with my immature emotions. It would show that victory is achievable and be used to start God discussions on healing the soul of a man while breaking down the barriers that destroy family unity.

In researching rejection, I've learned that we can choose to embrace the acceptance of God and refuse to allow wrong perceptions to dictate our lives. Two people who are willing to acknowledge pain, and put in the work to overcome it, can live harmonious lives together. I intentionally choose to think more optimistic thoughts than negative ones. I work toward managing my feelings rather than avoiding them. All the unanswered questions created feelings of inadequacy and insecurity. Therefore, rather than seeing myself as an orphan, unwanted, and unloved, I had to realize that I was loved, which also includes the love of self.

My wife is my anchor. Together, our purpose is coming into view. We have a contribution to make to the world, and it is a joy to do it together. I resolved to be a man of accountability and responsibility. As the head of my home and my marriage, it is my duty to lead with integrity. As we continue journeying together, we must have a vision for our marriage. Keeping ourselves tied to that vision will aid us to walk in wholeness and not venture off without regard for one another. I want my wife to be secure in our relationship. I know, without a doubt, she will follow my lead. I aim to make following me a pleasure rather than filled with uncertainty and pain. Having her respect gives me the courage to soar. She's been behind me 100% in searching for my biological parents. This has been an expedition filled with highs and lows. Having her shoulder to lean on has helped me unpack and process the pain as well as share in the joy of connecting with my blood relatives.

Marriage is God's design. It's His Holy covenant; therefore, it is not only my responsibility; it is my pleasure to honor God with my marriage. Seeing my precious wife as God's holy gift to me, helps me to cherish her more. We are not perfect, but we are perfect for one another. God commands that I love her as He loves the church. His Word says that He sanctifies and nourishes the church. As I grow more and more in love with her, washing her in the Word and honoring her with my actions brings me joy. Jesus gave Himself over for the church. His sacrifice is still incomprehensible today. It sets the precedent for how we are to love our wives. We've all heard it said that we cannot give what we haven't received. I've been blessed to be loved and embraced by two sets of family. More importantly, I've been blessed to be loved by God Himself. That alone gives me more than an ample amount of love to give to my wife.

My wife could have abandoned me a long time ago, but she chose to stay and fight for our covenant. I'm humbled by the resilience that she possesses. I value her and am working daily to live in a way that shows how much I am willing to sacrifice for her as God instructs us to do. In counseling, we've both learned that neither our responses nor behaviors should be based on one another's mistakes or mess-ups. They must be founded solely on Jesus Christ, who is our highest standard. Because of our love for Him, we ought to love one another and patiently work through any disagreements. True love is tested not in the easy pleasurable moments, but when a person is behaving like they least deserve it. This is just to say, we may not always get it right, but we are going to work through whatever comes. For with God all things are possible.

Retreating to her arms instead of isolation is still a work in progress. Brick by brick, the walls are slowly being removed. It's not a one-time fix, and you're done. Deliverance and healing must be consistent. Old habits can resurface. They can pop up when you least expect them. That is why consistently reading the word of God and being held accountable is crucial to wholeness. In addition to being around people who are positive and moving in the same direction. Tracing my roots contributed to a lot of present traumas over past issues. Now that the pieces have been put into place, the pain no longer has mastery over me. Letting go of the past gives me the strength to pursue the future confidently. I remind myself daily of all the progress I've made.

Anger, Anxiety, Depression, and Frustration

Who knew that depression is really anger turned inward? Most certainly not me. I saw my behavior, but my attempts at changing myself without opening myself to therapy was futile. Coming from a man who could not properly communicate with people, having to open up to a stranger took a lot. But I quickly saw the benefit of my vulnerability. I let my guard down and trusted the process. Depression and anxiety held me in their grips. I'd respond in verbal outbursts as well. At the right moment, I could literally go from zero to one hundred. My abusive tone and foul language made me an unpleasant person to be around and live with. Therapy helps me to properly convey my feelings and emotions. It is also helping me to deal with the repressed emotions that cause depression, frustration, anxiety, and explosive anger. I've never been a physically abusive person, but verbal abuse is equally damaging. My temper was another cause of my many relationship problems. I didn't properly process my feelings and internalizing everything from a faulty perception caused me to behave in ways that I am ashamed of today. I didn't know how to take a moment to see if my feelings were valid or not, I simply acted on them. Even in situations that demand anger, where it is completely legitimate and justifiable, anger can be distorted by how it is displayed.

Distorted perception also creates scenarios in our heads. As I mentioned above, I can perceive my wife's actions as vile when they are innocent. I ruined many other relationships because of faulty perceptions. Allow me to take a moment to apologize to the many women that I hurt with my immature and unprocessed pain. "I am sorry. If you ever find yourself reading this book, please forgive me. I also pray that you have worked through and are working through any issues that may have resulted from you being in a relationship with me."

During my first marriage, my children were more than likely privy to arguments and conversations that were not always handled properly; therefore, I also want to apologize to my children. "I ask you to forgive me also. I'm getting better, and that is my promise to you. When I fail, as I will, please know that humanity befalls us all. But I'm diligently determined to become a better man."

Having an open conversation after both parties have had time to calm down is necessary to gain understanding and insight into the other person's feelings. It is pride to always feel the need to be "right" or have the final say. Harmony isn't about winning an argument; it is more about coming to a mutual understanding. Coming to grips with the roots of my anger has helped me see that my anger wasn't about those that I was angry with, it was the voids in my life that left holes in my soul. My challenge now is working to find constructive methods of communication, rather than being destructive with my words and actions. Up until now, I prided myself on not leaving any crumbs so to speak. People always know where I stand and where I am coming from. If I needed to get a point across, I'd make sure they understood. I prided myself on speaking my mind. I understand now that this was also a defensive mechanism of rejection. I don't want to make light of my behavior; verbal abuse is still abuse. It's hard for me to process that and call myself an abuser, but for the sake of complete healing, I must be honest with myself.

Undisciplined anger leaves a person with loads of regrets. In fits of rage, we often say things that we will be sorry for later. In addition to hurting the person on the other end of the verbal assaults, it chips away at the self-esteem of the abuser. With my insecurities already heightened, exploding only made matters worse. I can't count the times, mornings, or evenings ruined by uncontrolled arguments. Unfortunately, children are often left to suffer in silence while listening to the screams and shouts coming through the walls. If not all, one of the children will inevitably inherit the same behavior.

Children model what they live. This is one reason that I cannot allow unproductive anger to coexist within the confines of my redeemed soul. My wife and I are working toward cultivating peaceful resolutions instead of making our home a war zone. Again, I must reiterate, at times, anger is unavoidable, but it is what we do with anger that makes or breaks us. In fact, it breaks all of those who are victims to it.

Let's discuss what I'm learning in managing anger. First, I must acknowledge the anger, hurt, and/or frustration. My family should not have to guess or figure it out based on my reactions. Going into a silent place was my comfort zone, but I am ridding myself of that. They should not witness my slamming doors or other objects. They shouldn't witness explosive shouting or abusive language. I can let them know that I need a moment to myself to properly process my emotions. Third, I must pray and convey my feelings to God. I must ask Him to take away the feelings of uncontrolled anger and give me His peace. I will need His help to see things clearly and ask Him to give me the words to respond in a way that brings Him glory. When I assess the situation, I may discover that the anger I feel is my issue and not the other person's. Therefore, they should not have to pay for what is wrong in my life. Fourth, fighting below the belt is never acceptable. Disagreements should never turn into a personal attack. e.g., name-calling, cursing, etc. Fifth, I'm learning that I should seek first to understand.

Honestly, it is very difficult to avoid saying what is on your mind or not to express what you are feeling. However, it isn't always wise. I have to practice just sitting in the moment, as the saying goes, "Think before you speak." Ask yourself, "Is my response going to be productive or constructive?" "Is what I am about to say going to destroy the other person?" Toxic behaviors are harmful, and the results always end in disaster. Proverbs 25:28 says, "A man without self-control is like a city without walls." That means a person who lacks self-control has no limits and no boundaries.

Walls in biblical times served as protection. Therefore, a city without walls is left unguarded and vulnerable to being conquered by the enemy. Self-control serves as that boundary to help us manage emotions. That brings me to my sixth point; there should be parameters; lines that we do not cross. Both parties must learn when an argument is over. We don't have to nag or insist that either of us be heard. It takes humility to say that it isn't a good time to discuss whatever issue it is but promise to talk about it later. One thing that I am going to practice is praying together to find a resolution before we talk things out. My wife is my partner, and at times even though I feel the weight of the world on my shoulder, I must be okay with allowing her to shoulder the world with me. It takes a lot, because I never want to feel like a failure, but I'm learning that admitting my need for help isn't failure, it's called being responsible.

Reconstructing the Foundation

Our physical lineage pales in comparison to our new spiritual lineage in Christ. Things that have been passed down or inherited are replaced by the heritage we have in God through Christ Jesus. Rebuilding starts with accepting what was, but determining that it does not have to be preserved. Just as my marriage is now founded with God at the core, I realized that I also needed to be rebuilt in God. I've determined that regardless of what I used to think of myself and what anyone else thought in the past, I am enough. Scripture says, "When I was a child, I spoke as a child, I understood as a child, I thought as a child, but when I became a man, I put away childish things."

The process to manhood, doesn't end at a certain age. Becoming is something we are all doing progressively. We've been taught to think our gender and extreme masculine traits are all it takes to be a man. We've been taught that crying and showing emotion outside of anger is less than a man should be. Consequently, these ideologies have caused men to suffer in silence and to manifest behavior in less than honorable ways. In 1 Corinthians 13:11, the Apostle Paul teaches that growth is progressive. And that progression must be purposeful. We must risk putting away behaviors that serve as comfortability and familiarity. To do that, it involves surveying our lives. Introspection is honestly examining or observing one's mental and emotional processes. Again, it is being honest about where we've been, where we are, and where we expect to go. Without honesty, any attempts to move forward will be ineffectual. Furthermore, Solomon, who is highly revered for the profundity of his words, issues a profound axiom in saying, "The race is not to the swift, nor the battle to the strong." He reveals that it takes great perseverance and determination to evolve. Every day is a new opportunity to make changes. It's time for us as men to reclaim what is rightfully ours. We are not here to fight statistics; we are here to create new paradigms. We must reset the standard and heal our families so that our legacy produces men of honor and women of respect.

Chapter Eight
Unprocessed Pain

I'd like to start this chapter by saying that I am not a counselor nor therapist. I am speaking from personal experience and the knowledge I've gained about wounds from the past. I understand that healing can't be time-stamped, although it should be progressive. Up until this point, this book has been primarily about my adoption journey, I pray this portion will not only be eye-opening but aid others in finding the closure and healing that is needed to avoid projecting past trauma onto others. As you have read in earlier chapters, meeting my blood family meant the world to me. I was excited to finally be able to connect all the dots and have this big beautiful, extended family, only to become the object or reminder of someone else's toxic behavior.

There were some things that transpired unbeknownst to me that when I came along caused certain family members to distance themselves from me. When I first connected to my family, I felt a remarkable sense of acceptance. I quickly realized that being blood does not have benefits; being blood has conditions. I found out about some transgressions that happened in earlier years. The pain they experienced had nothing to do with me, and it was also well before they knew of my existence.

Considering the gravity of the situation, my heart goes out to the victims; however, I am an innocent party. I wasn't a part of it, and had no knowledge of it, until the pain of their distance created questions. Their reaction to me was a clear sign that many suffer from unprocessed pain.

Most families tend to bury issues and keep secrets to avoid any confrontation, negative emotions, or ruining the family name. At times, people feel the sting of shame, regret, or dwell on how others will view them. Some refuse healing because they do not want to hurt others in the family. Therefore, instead they bury their stories, and secretly allow pain to eat away at their happiness. Our secrets can protect others, and simultaneously torment us. I asked the following questions, "How are you supposed to ever move on? Who is hurting other than yourself? And worse, who else will this hurt now or in the future?" In my case, it was hurting me.

I was told that some relatives didn't want to have a relationship with me because of what someone else did and somehow, I was a reminder of that pain. They felt that it would be better to keep me at a distance. I didn't understand what was going on. But eventually, another relative gave me more details. In addition to them, I also had a few other relatives who never responded to my calls or messages. I've waited 40 plus years to be united with my family only to be divided by matters that were beyond my control. The sting of rejection came rushing back into my soul.

Their pain wasn't my issue, and at the time, my own hurt overshadowed the fact that triggers for others can come just as easily as they can for me. In a few short months after our meeting, some of the family conversations and text stopped. I utilized all communication outlets, phone, text, and email, only to constantly be ignored. With everything I had already gone through, this was a huge blow for me. Healing is a process, and each person is responsible for taking the steps to live in wholeness. We've all heard that time heals all wounds. Time isn't the healer; but personal growth and self-reflection can facilitate healing. Trust me, it sounds easier than it is. Healing and its time frame can depend on the nature of the abuse, issue, or trauma. I've learned that it won't happen unless you take the necessary steps. Therapy is helping me to open up in ways I never thought I would.

I heard a bishop say that bitterness belongs to those who have decided not to heal. It is a decision that each of us must make because we've all had to overcome some things in life, even if the offense, pain, or circumstance isn't the same. I do understand that no two victims can be compared, so I won't attempt to compare. Also, to protect the victims, I'm doing my utmost not to mention the actual situations but offer any part of my testimony and aid towards some family resolution. I realize your testimony and experience are yours alone to share. I can't apologize or take the blame for what my family member did.

I was finally able to embrace this part of my biological family and learn of my past roots and identity. But because I bore a strong resemblance to their perpetrator, my identity was once again shattered. I was already working through the layers of hurt, and to have darts thrown at me for something I had nothing to do with hurt me to my core. My only fault was my DNA. Unfortunately, this happens in many households. A child that resembles or has the same mannerisms as the "hated" parent is often the object of the custodial parents' pain. A child should never have to be the receptor of such hate.

When a person notices triggers, the tendency is to avoid the person or things that trigger instead of trying to find a place of peace. This is in no way to imply that these individuals have not put in the work towards healing and I in no way intend to minimize or trivialize their pain. I'm sure they may have attempted to heal to a degree, but seeing me caused painful memories to resurface. Avoiding me will not erase those. The thing to do is to confront them head-on.

I know first-hand that forgiveness is one of the primary keys to healing. Family can be restored, and generational wholeness can happen when all parties are willing to heal, forgive, and work together to bridge gaps. We all hope for families that have mutual respect, genuine joy, and understanding. We often admire those who build and leave generational wealth. However, the fabric of the family is often torn apart and fractured by the lack of safety and dysfunction. Which can include abuse, harmful secrets, parental partiality, jealousy, and addictions.

Most children were raised by emotionally unavailable parents. I'm not saying this is their story, because I don't have all of the pieces. I am speaking from the wisdom I've gained in counseling, church, and the books I've studied. (I'm still walking out my own process), while learning how I can best help others. God has purpose in the pain. I'm not telling you not to sit in anger or frustration. Do that. I've heard it works wonders. Just don't allow it to dictate your life. You owe it to yourself not to put up a façade or fade into consistent despair.

Beware of shame. It makes us want to shut down or forces us to wear mask. Rather than allowing shame to win over you, accept help from others. The days when you don't want to be bothered, and you don't want to talk it out with a friend or therapist, just rest. Days when fear seems to grip your soul, and you feel overwhelmed, sit in it. Don't allow others, or even me, to rush your process. I'm working hard at understanding the pain that others must process and not make it all about me or what I desire to happen in my timing. Find a safe space to grieve, cry, and or rest. We all need safe spaces. Unfortunately, for many what we consider safety produces more damaging behavior, like drugs, overcompensating, overspending, rebellion, and the false security of someone's bed. Again, I'm not projecting, this is my attempt to help by what I've learned. I'm referring to a safe space as group therapy, or a group that allows you to just sit.

If you don't want to verbalize it, and all you want to do is be surrounded by people who have walked the same path, pray for that safe space. When you need a break, find a network of people to run the errands, cook the meals, or take you on a relaxing retreat. Remember asking for help is half the battle. I apologize if you have asked for help and didn't receive it because of someone else's denial. It is very difficult to face the fact that a person or the people they love could hurt or harm someone. I don't agree with denial.

As a parent, I've developed a strong sense of protection for my children. But I do know that no matter how hard I try to shield them from pain, the devil can at times still find his way to them. Your story has aided me in keeping my antennas high, and to remember not to become so occupied with my own healing that I am oblivious to any dangers. I hate what happened to you all.

A person who is supposed to protect, yet deny your pain, can compile the hurt. Denial can push a person deep into isolation. It can cause the victim to feel unheard and ignored. Many learn to dissociate from the painful experience because no one believed or appeared to care. I pray you hear me, "I care!" You have a right to speak about your experience and the right to heal.

To my family suffering any kind of mental anguish, if I can encourage you, please know that you've already survived what was meant to destroy you. You've overcome formidable odds, and God has placed on the inside of you all you need to move forward. This isn't simply a, "let it go" message or mantra, it's my heart pouring into yours. God is able to make all grace abound towards you once you surrender. In fact, future generations applaud your perseverance. Please take note of your strengths. If any of it produced negative cycles, stifled your growth, limited you or hindered you during any part of your life, if what you used to cope was unhealthy, this is your chance to stand up and say, "no more!" Trust that God will restore all that you've lost.

It pains me greatly to know that this horrendous act flowed through our bloodline. But, because of your courage, we have the awesome opportunity to cut it off at the head! We can rise up and declare that no more of our children and children's children will suffer this kind of action. We can reclaim our bloodline and declare like Joseph, "What the enemy meant for evil, God allowed, for the saving of many lives." I encourage you all to use your testimony to heal and aid others in healing. There are more books to be written, songs to be sung, organizations and foundations to form, parents to educate, and generations to raise. Like it or not, we are family. We don't get to choose who will be a part of that, we are simply born into it. And we can choose to be different.

Reconciliation takes time. Before I came to this realization, I wrote my feelings in the poem that you will soon read. I will go ahead and include it, as it helped me process the rejection that I internalized because of being shunned. Since writing it, I've grown by leaps and bounds. I based those words off the pain that I allowed the enemy to dump on me about you without knowing all of the facts, and without giving you the space that you needed to connect to me in your timing.

I apologize. Emotional maturity isn't developed overnight. We often see through the lenses of our own pain and what we hope or desire. It takes emotional strength to know that while we may not be the cause of pain, we can very well bear the brunt of it. It's easy to convince ourselves that others are losing out because we do not want to face the fact that, somehow, we feel that same sense of loss.

Denial is a strong cover-up for rejection. And as I've already transparently unmasked in the earlier chapters of this book, I removed the mask of denial now. I admit that I was hurt by your actions towards me. In trying to process this new level of grief for me, my cousin said, "You're not the person who hurt them." That was major to me! Although I knew that I wasn't the cause of their pain, his words were like a river of peace that flowed over my soul. It was hard to contain my emotions. In that moment of feeling rejected, I took that pain on as if it were in fact me. The anger that was directed towards me, by the refusal to communicate, embrace, and love me, led me back to that place of once again having to prove my worth. I felt myself drifting back into the shell that I've worked so hard to shed.

I'd heard many wonderful stories, but to be met with the unimaginable shattered those images. As I work to understand you all, I am still on my own healing journey. I'm confident in God that we will emerge stronger than ever. I was not the intentional object of your pain. My showing up out of the blue didn't give you time to prepare nor process the image you'd see. Yet I refuse to walk in shame. Journeying backwards sometimes will tarnish the reputations of those who've gone before us. It's a price that must be paid as living your truth will also bring healing. We must confront the ugliness to uncover the beauty. As my layers come off, I pray that everyone will see the benefit and the need for family wholeness. In my hurt, I composed the words you will read in the poem on the next few pages. From its length, you can tell my heart hurt as the words came pouring out of my soul. It was my method of self-preservation.

Your Loss

I had dreams of one day meeting
my biological family,
with the hopes that they would
except and treat me like their own.

Because when you look at it,
I was technically a part of them
but only to find out
just to some.

Maybe it was naïve of me to believe
that I would completely be accepted
only to be intercepted
by deceptive smiles
that concealed a pain that I was
unaware of.

I came in wide open
and vulnerable
not knowing anyone
only wanting to build relationships
with those who shared the same DNA
and hoping to catch up on time lost.

But I found out that later on
I would have the burden of carrying a cross
that I was unable to bear.

I was confused
because of the reaction to my existence
from one side of my family
was so authentic and genuine
that I believed that it would transcend
to the other side.

But I was sadly mistaken,
because there were those who did not want
the same thing I wanted
and that was just to make blood line
connections,
that would point me in the right direction.

But because of my reflection,
I was considered an infection,
and like Covid
they distanced themselves from me.

I believed that after our first conversation
that many would follow,
I imagined trips and get-togethers,
phone call conversations with family
but when I called, they didn't call back.

And what a smack in the face
to realize that when I text,
there was no response

and communication fell on hollow ears,
and I found that my presence
was too much to swallow.

What hurts is that they never
gave me a chance
to show them the real me.
They never gave me the chance
to show them that although
I didn't grow up with them,
I could grow with them,
and I could be an asset to the family.

But my thoughts
were not their thoughts and I fought
with the fact
that they felt it was fine
to distance themselves from me
and give me
the silent treatment without a reason.
So, I'm left with the disdain of a pain
that left a stain
that could not be erased
leaving me faced
with unforeseen trauma,
that has now become a part of my own.

So, I dealt with the hurt,
like I always have
And brushed it off with a smirk or a laugh.
And realized that at the end of the day
I am not the one who is missing out

It's you.

You decided that it was me
that you chose to toss,
therefore it's your loss.
I will keep it moving
and not shed another tear.

Your loss,

you won't get the chance to
meet my family
and those that I hold dear.

The healing you needed
could have come through me,

Maybe we will cross each other's path,
one day ... we will see.
I just wanted you to be a part of my world,
and that can't be.

Your loss,

Reggie

Conclusion

"We may have our differences, but nothing's more important than family."
–Coco

Writing this book has been both eye-opening and healing for me. Thank you for coming along with me on this journey. I've transparently shared some of the deepest, darkest moments of my life together with God's incredible grace towards me. I've come to realize that as we continue navigating the road of life and bridge the gaps within the family unit, we must, without fail learn to see our parents and other relatives as fallible human beings. The family circle is comprised of many people and many generations.

We may not fully understand what one individual has experienced to cause a particular behavior. That lack of understanding often leads to family conflict. Being able to properly handle conflict takes emotional intelligence. We don't learn that as infants. And until recently, I was not acquainted with the term. I understand that it is the capacity to be aware of, control, and express one's emotions, and to handle interpersonal relationships judiciously and empathetically.

The more we see our world, communities, and marriages decaying, the greater the motivation should be for us to build legacies, bridge relationships, and break negative cycles. Depending on where a person is in life and their willingness to grow, heal, and move forward; it is a task that will prove more daunting than effortless.

Maturation is a process; it doesn't necessarily come with age. Instead, it proceeds from a determination to create and foster a family built on the shoulders of those who stood before us. More importantly, on the design of the Master Builder, (GOD).

Knowing God's greatest desire is for generational wealth and wholeness in Him, is a phenomenal thing to behold. As we learn to forgive and forge our own paths, we have God's spirit aiding and even bidding us to change the trajectories of our futures and the future generations.

In His Grace,

– Reggie

Reginald A. Smith Jr. and Reginald A. Smith Sr.

APPENDICES

APPENDIX I
FAMILY SECRETS

Family secrets often can destroy the family foundation. Unfortunately, secrets pass down from generation to generation and eventually, rear their ugly head at the most inopportune time. In the case of my adoption and many other things, I along with so many others, have been the beneficiary of secrets that resulted in pain. Family secrets can be damaging and emotionally cataclysmic.

Families keep secrets for various reasons. One common motivation is protection, where secrets safeguard someone's privacy, well-being, or reputation. This can involve shielding family members from potential embarrassment, judgment, or harm by concealing sensitive information. Another reason is preserving harmony, as sharing certain secrets might lead to conflict or strained relationships, prompting families to maintain a façade of stability. Cultural and social stigma also play a role, in families that hide information to avoid judgment or discrimination. Fear of consequences, such as legal issues or damage to reputations can also lead families to keep secrets as a way of self-preservation.

Sometimes, families may feel that individuals are not emotionally ready, or the timing isn't right to reveal certain secrets, opting to wait until the circumstances are more appropriate. Additionally, family secrets can be perpetuated through generational patterns, where secrecy becomes a norm inherited from previous generations.

While some secrets may be kept with good intentions, it is essential to recognize the potential long-term consequences and prioritize open, honest communication to maintain healthy family relationships.

Family secrets can give rise to many significant problems within a family. One of the most significant issues is the erosion of trust. When important information is withheld from certain family members, it can create a sense of betrayal and resentment. When trust, which is crucial for healthy relationships, is compromised, it leads to strained dynamics and difficulty rebuilding broken bonds. Family secrets also contribute to a breakdown in communication.

When specific topics are off-limits or hidden, family members may hesitate to express themselves fully or share their thoughts and emotions. This lack of open communication can hinder the development of strong, meaningful connections within the family, leading to isolation and detachment. The emotional burden associated with family secrets is another major problem. Keeping a secret within the family can weigh heavily on those who are aware of the secret. And depending upon the nature of the secret, while they may protect one person, they leave others at risk, as in the case of a molester or rapist.

Feelings of guilt, anxiety, and shame can impact the mental health and well-being of those forced to keep secrets. The constant pressure to keep the secret can be overwhelming, and individuals may feel trapped in a cycle of secrecy and emotional distress. Family secrets also often result in inequality and division. When some family members are aware of the secret while others are kept in the dark, it creates a sense of exclusion and unequal distribution of information. This can breed resentment and sow discord within the family, leading to fractured relationships and further isolation. Interpersonal conflict is a common consequence of family secrets. When the truth eventually comes to light or suspicions arise, it can lead to arguments, confrontations, and damaged relationships. Resolving these conflicts often requires significant effort and time. Family secrets can also have a profound impact on an individual's identity. It may challenge preconceived notions and beliefs, causing confusion and emotional distress as individuals grapple with their sense of self and place within the family.

Finally, family secrets can have a generational impact. If information is intentionally hidden or distorted, it can affect the understanding and perception of family history. The lack of transparency and truth can perpetuate a cycle of secrecy, making it difficult for subsequent generations to form accurate narratives and establish a healthy family legacy. While not all family secrets are harmful, those that involve significant and pertinent information affecting multiple family members can lead to these major problems. Open and honest communication and a willingness to address and resolve family secrets are essential for fostering trust, maintaining healthy relationships, and nurturing a strong family unit.

APPENDIX II
ADOPTION

I've always wanted to adopt a child. I wanted to give back to the community of those who are in the foster care system. I want to be that twinkle of light and hope to give someone a loving home and the security of a family. In my line of work, I've seen firsthand the hurt, pain, neglect, and rejection that children experience in the system. Unfortunately, even after adulthood, many find it difficult to shake the feelings of unworthiness. I feel it would bring me a sense of joy and a different level of peace to know that I was a part of the process of helping to change lives and have them look at me the same way I looked at my parents.

Many of their stories are tragic, and although my heart is sensitive in this area, I do realize that I cannot adopt all of them, nor save them from every toxic environment by myself. But if God would grant me the stewardship of just one. I'd feel a sense of greater purpose and know that I have seeded a small portion into my unique destiny. It will really take the power of praying believers and a large community of people who understands how greatly adoption is needed in our country and the other nations of the earth.

I wanted to include this information in hopes that someone reading it, may benefit from knowing how many children, really are in need of loving families. But before I share the statistical information, let's read what God says regarding taking care of orphans and how this is a part of our Christian faith. James 1:27 says, "Religion that God our Father accepts as pure and faultless is this: to look after orphans and widows in their distress and to keep oneself from being polluted by the world."(NIV)

Adoption isn't ideal for everyone, but God does call us to sacrifice for the good of one another. There are also many opportunities to give [donate] to legitimate organizations that help orphans. If you choose this route, be sure to do complete research because scammers do exist. I'd hate for anyone to get taken advantage of while trying to do good. The statistics of children that are waiting to be adopted is alarming. Not many people or preachers teach or preach this part of the Bible.

Most importantly, it shows just how tender God's heart is towards widows and orphans. I do not want this portion to be about bashing the church, because I'm not. However, I do find it to be an overlooked part of the Bible. Sure, there are many church budgets and resources that include benevolence and giving to those less fortunate, yet still, not much talk is about taking care of orphans. In fact, adoption would lessen the statistical data of the unadopted and also please God. Amid all the planning, projects, and programs the church does, I pray that one day, we Christians would seek other ways to expend resources that align completely with the Word of God. Although we love to do good things for God, we can do even greater things when we consider what God desires from each of us.

We can see from the news reports how horrible thousands of foster care children are treated. Of the more than 400 children identified as victims of sexual abuse in 2021, the report found 25% were victimized in foster care or revictimized after entering foster care. The report notes that this is a "slight increase" from the Monitors' second report, filed May of 2021.

This isn't to say that all foster care parents are abusive or neglectful. There are many that foster successfully, and in many cases, it leads to them adopting the children after they have formed a strong bond. I am blessed to have been adopted early on, and in a very loving stable family. I also have a friend who was adopted. He was blessed as well to be raised in a very loving family.

Since writing this book, I've seen several stories break of those who have discovered that they were adopted. While the news isn't easy to hear, they have been blessed to be reared by those who loved them as their very own.

The most recent AFCARS report of the U.S. Department of Health and Human Services states that there are almost 114,000 foster children eligible and waiting to be adopted. In 2021, 54,200 foster kids were adopted which is a decline of approximately 3700 from the prior year. Although the number of adoptions has declined, the report found that for the past decade the percentage of children in foster care who are eligible for adoption has remained stable from 26-29%. Among these children, males outnumber females. On any given day, there are approximately 391,000 children in foster care in the United States.

In 2022, almost 214,000 children entered the U.S. foster care system, and infants represented over 70% of the total increase. Close to 60% of children in foster care spend two to five years in the system before being adopted. Almost 11% spend five or more years in foster care before being adopted. Unfortunately, there are some that are never adopted. It's heartbreaking, however, there are many factors to consider in adopting a child. I've listed some of those factors below:

Motivation and Readiness: The first consideration is the motivation and readiness of the prospective adoptive parents. It is essential to ensure that they are emotionally, mentally, and financially prepared to adopt a child and provide a stable and loving home.

Type of Adoption: There are different types of adoption, including domestic, international, open, and closed adoptions. Prospective adoptive parents should consider which type of adoption is best for their family and research the requirements and regulations involved.

Age of the Child: The child's age is another critical factor to consider. Adopting an older child may require different parenting skills than adopting a younger child. Parents should also consider their own ages and the ages of any other children in the household.

Health and Medical History: Parents should consider any potential health and medical issues that the child may have and whether they are prepared to provide the necessary care and support.

Cultural and Ethnic Background: If adopting a child from a different cultural or ethnic backgrounds, parents should consider how they will support the child in maintaining a connection to their culture and community.

Legal and Financial Considerations: Adoption involves legal and financial considerations, such as the cost of adoption, legal requirements, and potential risks and liabilities.

Support Systems: Prospective adoptive parents should consider their support systems, such as family, friends, and community, and whether or not they will have the necessary emotional and practical support to navigate the adoption process and provide a stable home for the child. They should also do as much research as possible to prepare themselves for the possibility that the child may eventually want to locate their biological parents. They should have that right. Also consider the emotional impact of being put up for adoption, the foster care system, and any other behavior issue that may need to be dealt with.

Adopting a child is a major decision. It is one that requires careful consideration of various factors to ensure that the child's needs are met. The parents must be prepared to be open and honest with the child or children. While the adoption process is sometimes arduous, the results are immeasurable. Whether you're bringing your first child into your family, or adding to a growing one, the feeling of joy is the same. Your days will be a little brighter, and your future more promising when you add a new bundle of joy to your life.

When it comes to adopting a child, it's hard to put into words what you will gain from making the decision. Every parent is unique, and the benefits will vary from family to family. Just know that the rewards will outweigh the fears.

Notes

Chapter 5

1. https://en.wikipedia.org/wiki/Six degrees accessed 01.18.24

Appendices

1. "7 Dangers of Keeping Family Secrets." Amen Clinics 7 Dangers of Keeping Family Secrets Comments, 5 July 2021, www.amenclinics.com/blog/7-dangers-of-keeping-family-se-crets.
2. "US Adoption Statistics: Adoption Network." Adoption Network |, US Adoption Attitudes Survey Conducted by The Harris Poll on behalf of the Dave Thomas Foundation 2024 Copyright Adoption Network, Feb. 2022, adoptionnetwork. com/adoption-myths-facts/domestic-us-statistics/#:~:text=How%20many%20children%20are%20available,and%20waiting%20to%20be%20adopted.
3. James 1:27 New Living Translation.
4. Psych Central, MentalHelp.net, Psychology Today, Focus on the Family, BBC Future, Power of Positivity
5. https://www.kxan.com/investigations/report-more-children-abused-or-revictimized-after-entering-texas-foster-care/#:~:text=Of%20the%20more%20than%20400,second%20report%2C%20filed%20last%20May.
6. https://adoptionnetwork.com/adoption-myths-facts/domestic-us-statistics/
7. https://www.all4kids.org/news/blog/the-benefits-of-adopting-a-child/

BIOGRAPHY

Reginald A. Smith, affectionately known as Reggie, was born on November 3rd, 1972, in Gary, Indiana. From the very beginning Reggie was embraced by a loving middle-class family who provided him with a nurturing and supportive environment. Throughout his life, Reggie excelled both in sports and education, showcasing his determination and passion for personal growth. Currently, he is pursuing his Doctorate degree, a testament to his unwavering commitment to academic excellence. In addition to his academic pursuits, Reggie finds fulfillment in his roles as a husband and father.

He is happily married to his wife, Diana L. Smith, and together they have five children: Reggie Smith Jr., Taleah Redd, Tiyona Wright, Dominique Williams, and Derrick Redd Jr. His family has expanded with the arrival of three grandchildren. He looks forward to more grandchildren that will add to the joy and love in their lives. Reggie's passions extend beyond his academic and family life. He has a deep love for training athletes, helping them unlock their full potential and achieve their goals.

Additionally, Reggie finds solace and creative expression in writing poetry, where he captures the essence of his emotions and experiences through words. Reggie's commitment to serving others is evident in his 20 plus years of dedicated service in the social and human services sector, particularly in the field of mental health. He also served 8 1/2 years in the U.S. Navy and Army. His invaluable contributions have positively impacted the lives of countless individuals, demonstrating his compassion and dedication to making a difference. Reggie currently resides in Southern California and continues to pursue his passions, support his family, and make a meaningful impact in the lives of others through his work in mental health and through his creative endeavors.